Sourdough

Riccardo Astolfi

Sourdough

A Complete Guide and Recipe Book

Guido Tommasi Editore

CONTENTS

For Zeno and Alfonsina,
who met only
for a second

Making bread is an act that reconnects us with the past, with former generations, our grandparents and great-grandparents, reminding us of who we are along a journey of rediscovery. At the same time, making bread is an activity replete with hope, joy, renewal and progress towards the future. It requires know-how and the patience to keep vigil in order to create something simple yet rich and wholesome for one's family, friends, and one's self.

Kneading bread is a ritual in itself, one of sober and calculated gestures and slow, rhythmic dexterity. Like a vibrant, undulating dance, kneading turns basic ingredients like flour, water, and starter into a unique and complex dough, in perfect symmetry and balance.

Making bread with sourdough starter means reconnecting with the Earth, with the land, with peasant culture and traditions. It's also an opportunity to support local biodiversity and organic production while helping to conserving the environment for future generations.

A physical—and especially spiritual—practice, making homemade bread requires understanding of elements like times and limits. It requires listening to a rising dough and a loaf of bread as it bakes, noticing its shape, aromas, flavors and colors.

In much the same way, breadmaking is also about understanding our own times, our own limits, and learning how to listen to and observe ourselves.

Homemade bread offers us a chance to enjoy the beauty and gifts all around us. Give some of your extra starter to others, even strangers, and in return you'll receive an unexpected bounty in the form of a flower, a head of garden lettuce, or a jar of homemade jam. And a smile.

It's my wish that each of us can experience the joy, surprise, curiosity and pure satisfaction that a loaf of fresh-baked bread brings.

Happy reading, and happy baking.

WHAT IS SOURDOUGH?

A sourdough starter is nothing more than a simple mixture of flour and water in which the fermentation processes characteristic of leavening are triggered, thanks to the different types of microorganisms found in flour and in the surrounding environment: yeasts and bacteria that live within bread doughs and feed on the sugars present, transforming them primarily into gas (carbon dioxide).
Sourdough starter can be used to leaven dough for bread, pizza, focaccia, and leavened cakes in much the same way as baker's yeast (dry or fresh). This is a more complex type of leavening, requiring more time and greater attention, yet it will also yield very satisfying results.

CREATING A SOURDOUGH STARTER

Unlike commercial baker's yeast, a sourdough starter will not be available in your average supermarkets, not even organic markets.
Once in a while you might come across a packet of dried sourdough on store shelves (see page 35), but these products are composed of natural yeasts that have undergone invasive dehydrating, freeze-drying, and grinding processes that deactivate the fermenting qualities of yeasts and bacteria. They may add aroma, but they nonetheless require the addition of baker's yeast to leaven.

The simplest way to obtain sourdough starter is to receive some as a gift. Ask your friends or your trusted baker to give you a bit of theirs. Otherwise try searching online for associations like Italy's Cibo Pasta Madre (www.pastamadre.net), which provides a free map for sourdough starter "dealers", people who are happy to donate a small piece of their own starter to those who ask.

Certainly the greatest satisfaction will come from growing your own from scratch, creating life in the form of a small amount of starter with little more than a bit of flour and some water.

Because sourdough is a mixture of yeasts and bacteria brimming with surprisingly high biodiversity levels, starters can be very different from one another, depending on factors like hydration and the flour used. A starter can be solid or liquid, made with wheat, rye or other grains, or using apple peel, yogurt, dried fruit, honey, or malt.

What we hope to provide here is a set of fast and easy instructions to follow in creating a sourdough starter at home. As mentioned, the variables are many, and thus there's no one way to perform this magic.

Before beginning, note the principle rule in making a sourdough starter and all subsequent doughs we will create in our careers as homemade breadmakers: ensuring the good living conditions for yeasts and lactic acid bacteria through feedings and warmth, the two main requirements for a starter to "live well."

RECIPE FOR CREATING A SOURDOUGH STARTER

Step 1:
Ingredients
100 g (¾ cup) organic all-purpose wheat flour
50 ml (¼ cup) water, room temperature
1 tsp organic honey

Honey helps to kick off fermentation in dough. Comprised of sugars simpler than those starches, honey is an easier feeding source for yeasts and lactic acid bacteria present in the flour and surrounding environment.
Furthermore, honey—especially organic or biodynamic—is a living product itself, rich in enzymes and micro-nutrients, able to lend pep and vitality to your dough.
Naturally you can substitute honey with other types of fermentation starters (see Other Fermentation Starters on the opposite page).

WHY CHOOSE ORGANIC?

Choosing ingredients sourced from organic producers is a good habit to get into along your homemade breadmaking journey, as organic products bring several considerable advantages in terms of our health, our environment, and our starter.
Not using pesticides in the field, not putting additives in flours and other ingredients, respecting the cultivation while simultaneously benefitting local and ancient grain varieties—in all these ways, organic farming and organic products are fundamental considerations for those who wish to make good, pure, fair and ethical bread. Moreover, organic products tend to be more "alive" since they contain a greater concentration of vital micro-nutrients and enzymes—important, if not fundamental, in creating and maintaining a sourdough starter.

WHY CHOOSE WHOLE WHEAT FLOUR?

With respect to more refined flours, whole wheat and semi-whole wheat flours are richer in enzymes and nutritional substances. An all-purpose, organic, semi-whole wheat flour will give your starter a good dose of the enzymes, yeasts and bacteria present in the grains.

OTHER FERMENTATION STARTERS

Adding simple sugars when you first begin your starter can help speed up the fermentation process. The following ingredients can be used in place of honey:
- Whole cane sugar
- Barley malt or other grain-based syrups (such as rice or corn syrup)
- Maple syrup
- Agave syrup
- Cane sugar molasses
- Concentrated apple juice
- Whole yogurt
- Grated apple peel
- Chopped raisins
Add a teaspoon to the starter.

Thoroughly knead all the ingredients together until a small, soft, smooth ball forms. Place this first dough in a bowl and cover with a damp towel. Let rest at room temperature for 48 hours.
After resting, the dough will be slightly puffed up, and you will note the appearance of the first bubbles.
If you don't see this activity, however, do not worry. Move on the the next step.

Step 2:
100 g (3.5 oz) of the starter made above
100 g (¾ cup) organic all-purpose wheat flour
50 ml (¼ cup) water, room temperature

After having removed any surface crust on the first starter dough, temper it with the water and, once smooth, add the flour. Continue in this manner until a new, well-structured dough forms.
You've just completed what's called "feeding" the starter—that is, you've provided your yeasts with a fresh batch of simple sugars (see *Maintaining and Feeding* on the page opposite).
Cover and let rest for another 48 hours.

Next steps:
Continue this feeding process (step 2) for at least two weeks, always keeping your starter at room temperature in a bowl covered with a damp towel, until it is able to double in volume in about 4 hours.

This usually requires at least a couple of weeks. Naturally, much will depend on the quality of the flours used, the climate and room temperatures, the bacterial microflora present in the air inside our homes. Depending on all these factors, fermentation can take off very quickly or can take longer.
In the first case, you can proceed immediately to baking your first breads. If, however, your starter is slow to ferment, continue to feed it. Don't despair—fermentation will happen sooner or later.

Once this process is complete, the starter is ready to be used to make bread. Keep the starter in a glass jar. It can be stored in the refrigerator in between feedings for more than a week. Use your judgement and foresight for best results.

MAINTAINING AND FEEDING A SOURDOUGH STARTER

Once you have created a starter (or been gifted one by a "dealer" friend), it's ready to be used to make homemade breads. Only a small amount needs to be kept, about 150-200 grams (or 5-7 ounces).

When not being used, keep it in the refrigerator in a glass jar or plastic container with a lid, for up to a full week. Do not close the jar lid tightly, but rather leave it slightly ajar, with the lid balanced on top to not let too much air in.

In this way the dough will breath (fermentation being predominantly aerobic), but at the same time the surface will not dry out too much.

Keep the starter alive by simply feeding it regularly, at least once a week. Let's see how.

The feeding process
150 g (5 oz) of sourdough starter kept in the refrigerator (1 part starter)
100 g (¾ cup) organic all-purpose wheat flour (1 part flour)
70-75 ml (⅓ cup) room temperature water (½ part water)

Dilute the starter in the water and once it is smooth add the flour. Knead thoroughly until a smooth, uniform mixture forms.

Cover and let rise at room temperature until double in volume (about 4-6 hours).

After this step, your starter is ready to be put to use in baking. Remove the quantity called for in your recipe, keeping a portion (about 100-200 grams or 3.5-7 ounces) in the jar in the refrigerator for future use. It easily keeps for 7-10 days.

If a recipe calls for a larger amount of starter than you have available, you can add more flour and water during feeding (the amount of water to add is usually half the weight of the flour).

If, on the other hand, you don't have any recipes planned to use up your starter, just keep feeding it weekly to keep it alive, and after it rises to room temperature each time, return it to the refrigerator to keep. Extra, unused sourdough starter can be given away or used in fast and easy recipes, as to not waste it.

In the beginning, each feeding will result in about 150 g (5 oz) of extra starter. In this early phase, providing a regular supply of fresh nourishment to the yeasts and bacteria is crucial.
But you don't have to toss out the excess starter. On the contrary. Give it to friends or relatives eager to start their own homemade bread adventures, or create some fast and easy snacks to "recycle" excess starter rather than waste it.

Roll out the excess dough to a thin, round layer and cook in a pan for a few minutes on each side, like an Italian *piadina* (similar to a flour tortilla). Season with olive oil, salt, spices, honey or jam. You have just made a snack without spending anything extra. But more importantly, you've not wasted the living starter.

IS YOUR STARTER HEALTHY?

A sourdough starter is typically considered "ripe" or "mature" when it's able to double in volume in 4-5 hours after a feeding.
As you can easily guess, the more your starter is used, the more balanced and active the microflora inside will be and the better it will ferment.
Additional characteristics of a healthy sourdough starter include:
- Look: ivory white, without mold or turning to grey; soft with small, uniform, elongated bubbles.
- Smell: balanced, slightly sour but not sharp or acetic.
- Flavor: similar to bread dough, pleasant, slightly sweet-sour, balanced.

BATH

STRENGTHENING A SOURDOUGH STARTER AND IMPROVING ACIDITY

If your starter is not very ripe, if it tends to turn acidic too quickly, develops an acetic and pungent odor, or has a sour taste tending towards bitter and a grayish color, there are ways to help restore it to its optimum state. This involves reducing acidity and revitalizing the microflora. How?

Bath (if the starter is too "strong" and sour)
- Cut the starter into slices and immerse in a bowl of tepid water (max 35° C/100° F), adding a spoonful of organic cane sugar.
- Wait 20-30 minutes, until some or all (or possibly none) of the slices float to the top of the water.
- Remove the floating pieces of starter and toss out those that remained at the bottom of the container. Proceed with feeding the starter, using the following quantities: 1 part starter, 1 part water, 2 parts flour.
- Continue the feedings every day until your starter is able to double in volume in 4 hours and shows the characteristics of a healthy, ripe starter like those described above.

More frequent feedings (for a starter that is too "weak")
A sourdough starter that lacks good alveoli (air bubbles), is not sour enough or almost sweet, that smells of flour and above all lacks strong fermentation activity is considered a "weak" sourdough.
To redress this sad state, you will have to feed your starter more frequently (once a day), using the following

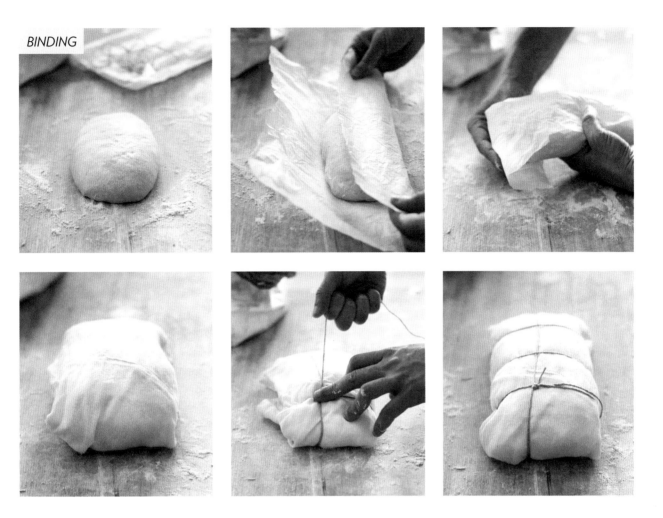

quantities: 2 parts starter, 1 part flour, ½ part water. Try to keep the starter at a temperature close to 26-28°C/79-82° F.

Once the starter can double in volume in about 4 hours, you have successfully strengthened your starter.

Binding (to boost fermentation)

Binding boosts fermentation and is often called for in rich, complex doughs like those used in leavened cakes. This visually enticing method is primarily used by professionals, but it can be done at home with little difficulty.

Before binding, make sure you have a good dose of starter (at least 300-400 g /10.5-14 oz). This is fundamental, as during the binding process the outer surfaces of the starter tend to dry out and become unusable. Some will have to be thrown out, and you will end up using only the inside portions before proceeding with feedings and making subsequent doughs.

- Transfer the starter to a sheet of baking paper, roll it into an oblong loaf shape, and wrap in a clean, unscented linen or cotton cloth (the baking paper will keep the dough from sticking to the cloth).
- Secure the shape with twine or a plastic band (as if it were a roast) but not too tightly. Let rest at room temperature for at least 4 hours before returning to the refrigerator.
- With fermentation, the starter will grow in volume and be held together with the well-secured twine. This will stimulate the sourdough when it's later untied.

KEEPING YOUR SOURDOUGH STARTER FOR LONG PERIODS

When you are not able to use your starter for baking, or when for long periods you won't be able to feed it, try to store it dried or keep it in the freezer.

If you will not be away for very long, however, trusting your starter to a friend or relative who can feed it weekly on your behalf is always a better option, as drying or freezing your starter can impact its health and microfloral balance.

Drying

Break your starter into pieces and place them in the beaker cup of a wand mixer, together with an equal quantity of flour. Process the mixture until a powder forms.

Spread the powder onto a baking sheet lined with baking paper and dry at room temperature for 3-4 days, mixing periodically. With most of the residual moisture removed from the dough, it will keep dried in a glass jar for a few months.

When you want to use it again, re-activate the starter by adding water and begin regular feedings again (once a day) until the starter is able to double in volume in the usual 4-6 hours.

Freezing

Transfer the sourdough starter to a glass jar or freezer bag, close well and keep in the freezer.

Sourdough preserved in this way will keep for a few months. When you want to use it again, it's important to bring it to room temperature first, then proceed with daily feedings until it gets back its former vitality—doubling in volume in 4-6 hours.

STANDARD PROPORTIONS AND GENERAL RULES

Baking with sourdough starter requires attention and dedication, but also a good dose of improvisation, the know-how to recognize when not to rely on the rules too much.

With experience, every home baker will improve his or her creations, graduating from a slavish adherence to recipes such as those contained in this book to their own adaptations and improvements, and eventually to the creation of their very own original recipes.

Being familiar with standard proportions will help bakers to understand the characteristics of recipes and breads even before they get their hands on the dough.

As we've already seen, the methods involved in creating and feeding sourdough starter require precise proportions (barring particular problems, these are: 1 part sourdough, 1 part flour, and ½ part water), and the same is true for making bread—which obliges the home baker to take out a calculator to analyze the different percentages of each required ingredient.

To begin, the baker's percentage principle must be understood. In the world of breadmaking, whether artisanal or industrial, calculations are proportional to the amount of flour used.

This means that the amount of flour used will be indicated at 100%, and that all other percentages for additional ingredients will be calculated in relation to the quantity of flour.

Let's take this example. We'll analyze the ingredients called for in the recipe for an einkorn wheat loaf:
150 g (5.3 oz) of fed starter
500 g (5 cups) einkorn wheat
250 ml (1 cup) water
2 tsp salt

By comparing these amounts to the amount of flour, we have the following percentages:
100% einkorn flour
30% fed starter
50% water
1-2% salt

Here is a table of the proportions of base ingredients called for in breadmaking:

Ingredient	Percentage
Flour	100%
Water	45 - 80% depending on the desired product and flour quality
Starter	15 - 30%
Oil or other fats	0 - 10% if called for
Salt	0 - 2% depending on taste and need

Note that this table should serve only as a starting point, to help bakers understand and plan recipes. Depending on the type and quality of ingredients used, and above all keeping in mind the final product you are trying to obtain, different proportions can be used, along with new and different ingredients (see *Other Ingredients* on page 24).

Understanding proportions and percentages can frighten the novice baker, and might even seem unnecessary at the beginning. Over time, however, this knowledge will prove very useful in comparing and adjusting different recipes, in improving and adapting them according to nutritional, flavor, and even organizational needs.

HYDRATION: HOW CAN A DROP OF WATER AFFECT BREAD

As often happens in cooking, the simplest and seemingly least important ingredient can in fact be a recipe's main protagonist, able to significantly affect the final results. In breadmaking, water plays a fundamental role.

The quantities of other ingredients being equal, by changing the amount of water added to the dough, we can create both hard-crusted traditional breads and softer, moist breads with excellent crumb and volume.

Furthermore, greater quantities of water in a dough can result in more yeast and bacterial activity, improving and speeding up the fermentation process.

Note that this does not mean that bread containing high amounts of water (above 60-70%) will be better than a drier hard bread (water less than 50%), but it will certainly produce a spongier and more elastic bread. If that is your goal, then try to increase the amount of water in your dough as much as possible.

Obtaining very hydrated doughs is not exactly easy, however. In fact, it's not merely a matter of adding water during the kneading phase, but rather this step requires skillful management, to make sure the water is completely absorbed by the flour's starches and glutens.

Naturally, this does not depend alone on a breadmaker's skill and ability (or the technical ability of his or her mixer).

Several factors influence how a dough absorbs water, the main ones concerning the flour used:

- type of flour: the stronger and more rich in glutens a flour is, the better it will absorb water.
- type of milling: when equal in strength, less-refined flours tend to absorb more water in the dough, as they are richer in bran.

FLOURS ALWAYS DIFFER: TYPES OF FLOURS AND GRAINS

Before your passion for breadmaking began, most likely your shopping list included the generic term "flour". Now, however, your curiosity will grow almost daily, as will your experimentation with different raw materials in the quest for an excellent bread. Do not be surprised if you start to become a bit obsessive when it comes to choosing a flour.

In this matter as with sourdough starters themselves, it's important to start with a general axiom: not all flours are the same.

Even two flours obtained from the same grain variety and grown in the same place can differ, depending on the land, the climate, storage conditions and milling.

Knowing how to "listen to" flours while kneading them with a starter is the best way to understand their true natures. For this reason, advising or providing opinions on a certain type of flour brand (or noted mill) is difficult. Leaving aside for now all grains other than soft wheat (which we will discuss later), the first aspect of flour to consider when choosing is its refining, more precisely called "sifting grade".

Types of flour	Nutritional profile	Baking characteristics
Type 00, or "doppio zero" in Italian (a very soft, fine white flour, similar to all-purpose flour)	Rich in starches (complex carbohydrates), low in nutritional value and micronutrients, fat content (wheatgerm) and almost no fiber.	Made for cakes, donuts, pastries, and "fresh" pastas. Completely unsuitable for leavened products for both its scarce fermentation capacity and its lack of nutritional value.
Type 0 (slightly less refined than type 00, similar to strong all-purpose or bread flour)	High starch levels, low levels of fats and fiber.	Used in making "white" breads, and a good compromise when just starting out in the world of breadmaking, before moving on to richer, whole-grain breads.
Types 1 and 2: semi-whole grain	Good fiber levels, more varied and complex both nutritionally and flavor-wise.	Lend a rich, decided flavor to breads, along with a golden color and crunchy crust. Excellent nutritional value, for breads not too heavy or moist.
Whole grain	Obtained from milling the entire grain kernel, rich in fiber, and if stone ground containing the wheat germ as well, the fat-containing part of the grain, aromatic and nutritionally more interesting. It's fundamental in this case to choose organic flours.	If milled correctly (stone-ground), results in extraordinary flavor complexity without impeding healthy leavening. Mixing with white flour with bran can weigh down the bread and result in poor, unbalanced taste.

It goes without saying that the more whole-grain the flour, the richer in healthy micronutrients and more flavorful the bread.

At the same time, it's just as important to choose organic, stone-ground flours in order to reduce, or even better eliminate altogether, the presence of pesticides and chemical residue. This will mean a nutritionally complete final product that contains all the bran and wheat germ (which is only possible with stone-grinding).

When it comes to commercial flours on the market, another important aspect to consider is alveolation, the technical and physical performance of a flour once it has been used to make bread: its strength, how resistant and elastic the dough is, and the amount of hydration it can sustain.

These are measurable factors that indicate strength (W) and the relationship between strength and elasticity (P / L). While these factors have always been considered by professional and industrial breadmakers, analyzed and listed in the technical data sheets of flours used in those contexts, only recently have home bakers started to consider them as well.

Given that this information is rarely made available to consumers who purchase commercial flours (only in isolated cases, in truth), and that rarely is a flour of the kind used outside the professional-industrial baking world able to sustain technical characteristics consistently from production batch to production batch, home bakers are left with two "mere" methods to rely on to truly understand the flours being used.

This first is experience. This is undoubtedly the more challenging route, yet once your skills are sharpened, it will become the best and most reliable method.

The second is hidden behind the word "Manitoba", which, contrary to a common misconception, does not indicate the grain's region of origin, but rather the flour's basic characteristics: identified namely as "strong" and thus able to withstand long leavening periods (certain cakes, for instance) and absorb more water (for breads with high hydration percentages). Today, flours of this kind are very common, appearing in television programs and cookbooks, but they are overrated. Remember, too, that these flours are rich in gluten (difficult to digest and possible causes of intolerance or sensitivity) and should be limited to cases of extreme necessity. So, in order to make the best bread possible, while not overlooking the various ethical, social, nutritional and flavor aspects involved, we should always follow a few fundamental points:

Organic

To some, choosing organic seems trendy, or a waste of money, but in fact organic (or biodynamic) flours offer a way to not only respect the environment and natural world, but also a means to support agricultural methods with lower environmental impact, those that do not use pesticides or invasive chemical treatments on land and crops. What's more, choosing organic flour is a way to show respect for ourselves, our health and our sense of taste while ensuring a healthy final product, one that is authentic, complex, with richer aroma and flavor.

Stone ground

How a flour is milled has an important influence in breadmaking. The typical "cylinder" industrial grinding method subjects the wheat grain to several invasive steps that strip it of its vitality and nutritional value, reducing flour to an ingredient void of flavor and substance, one considered only in terms of production yield.

Stone grinding, on the other hand, respects and enhances the grain's primary characteristics, transforming it into flour through a slow process that sustains its fundamental flavor and nutritional qualities. Stone-ground flour contains the internal part of the grain (the germ, rich in "good" fats) and the external part (the important bran fibers).

Ancient and local grains

Years of research and studies on grains in the agricultural industry have led to the development of new grain varieties, highly productive and designed for an agricultural system that uses pesticides and chemical fertilizers. These grains may be very productive, yet they lack flavor and also contribute to the increase of problems such as gluten intolerance and celiac disease, given their nutritional profile. Ancient grains, on the other hand, are richer in flavor and decidedly more balanced from a nutritional perspective. Moreover, due to their higher adaptability to land and their more "rustic" nature, they require less water and other resources, thereby reducing environmental impact. For all these reasons, buying local flours and grains shortens the supply chain and contributes to sustaining local economies, while often being easier on the wallet, too. What's more, getting to know the producers and millers who provide us with these products establishes a human connection, a relationship that over time can only benefit the quality of flour we use and the bread we make.

Beyond common wheat

Spelt, corn, buckwheat, einkorn wheat, rye, millet. So many grains beyond wheat exist that we can use for making breads and other baked goods. The recipes in this book call for different types of flours, to encourage experimentation with new ingredients to produce unusual and tasty breads. Let yourself be drawn into the fascinating world of grain biodiversity by trying out the many different flours available and adapting them to your taste and needs.

Spelt and rye flour are now considered common flours, and breads made from them easy to find in bakeries and even in supermarkets, but the same cannot be said of flours made from grains like millet, oats, and einkorn—uniquely flavored grains, rich in nutrients.

Below is a short table of basic information on different flours, their characteristics, and uses (whether using them 100% or adding to stronger wheat flours high in gluten).

The beneficial nutritional qualities of different grains depend on several variables (such as variety, cultivation, soil, milling method, and so on). The table here simply notes some of the flavor characteristics, to avoid misleading consumers, making false claims or promoting certain nutritional values over others.

Flour	Use (complete or partial)	Qualities
Durum wheat	Complete or partial	Warm color and intense aroma. Ideal for large loaves, as it lends bread a soft inside and crunchy, dark crust.
Spelt	Complete or partial	Lends bread the slightly dark color and rustic flavor characteristic of country breads.
Einkorn wheat	Complete or partial	With its particularly interesting nutritional profile (rich in proteins and fats, low in glutens), this flour is ideal for flavorful whole grain breads.
Buckwheat	Partial, with other stronger flours	Gluten-free. Lends breads the trademark grayish color and "peasant" flavor typical of mountain breads.
Millet	Partial, with other stronger flours	Gluten-free, pleasantly golden with sweet notes, this flour is perfect for lending an extra hint of color and flavor to breads and leavened cakes.

Flour	Use (complete or partial)	Qualities
Oat	Partial, with other stronger flours	Nutritionally very rich, this flour gives bread a robust flavor, but it tends to weigh down doughs: use in only smaller proportions.
Corn	Partial, with other stronger flours	Depending on the variety and milling method, can result in very soft, light breads, golden and pleasingly crunchy.
Rye	Complete or partial	A superb flour in mountainous areas that creates dark, aromatic, moist breads with a dense crumb. Usually combined with herbs and spices to enhance flavor and digestibility.
Chestnut	Partial, with other stronger flours	A common flour in the Italian countryside, the Apennine Mountains and forests. Use for slightly sweet round breads with a hint of smoke and a taste that recalls "mountain life".
Chickpea	Partial, with other stronger flours	Used on its own for traditional unleavened products like *farinata* (a pancake made from chickpea flour) and *panelle* (chickpea flour fritters), when added to breads in small percentages lends crunch, a toasted flavor and golden crust.
Rice	Partial, with other stronger flours	Gluten-free, white in color and light in consistency, this flour is ideal for creating soft and fluffy small breads and cakes.
Barley	Partial, with other stronger flours	A very rustic and unrefined flour that tends to weigh down doughs, but when used in small quantities results in a strong caramel flavor.

THE RECIPES IN THIS BOOK

With this book, I have tried to provide the reader with a complete picture of the infinite possibilities of sourdough breadmaking. To do this, I focused on recipes that require different types of flours and grains: from whole-grain to refined, classic wheat to einkorn wheat and on to durum wheat.

Naturally, as already noted several times, it will be up to the reader to try the recipes, evaluate them, and adapt them to their own specifications after attaining a good level of experience.

The suggestions in the paragraph on flours must therefore be considered a starting point, a reference to return to when you find yourself standing before a store shelf (or, better still, before a miller or farmer), attempting to sort out the choices of flour.

Every breadmaker should feel free to choose the type of flour that satisfies in both flavor and nutrition.

OTHER INGREDIENTS: SUGARS, FATS, SEASONINGS, LIQUIDS, AND WATER

The various ways to enrich bread with other ingredients are nearly endless. Whether you are vegan, omnivore, lovers of cheese or other particular items, you have countless ingredients at your disposal to transform your loaves into sweet or savory goods worthy of a master baker. No list of these extra ingredients would ever be complete. A more interesting consideration then is how to achieve certain results in our dough and bread by adding specific ingredients. The following table lists some of the most common ingredients to add to doughs, with simple notes on the technical and chemical-physical function carried out during baking, together with examples for each type.

Type of ingredient	Effect on dough and bread	Examples
Sweetener	In savory items, a small amount of added sugar can jump-start the fermentation process. In baking, sugars encourage lovely brown, crunchy crusts. In leavened cakes, sugars are one of the main ingredients and as such are added in larger quantities (about 10 to 40%). In this case, differently from leavened salted breads, a high percentage of sugar can actually slow leavening, so it's a good idea to add them halfway through the kneading.	Raw cane sugar, barley malt syrup, rice syrup, corn syrup, agave syrup, maple syrup, cane sugar molasses, honey.
Oils and fats	While not fundamental to classic bread recipes, oils and fats can be important or even essential ingredients to obtain more elastic, rich, crispy or crunchy breads (such as focaccia). Typically salted breads call for extra virgin olive oil in quantities ranging from 5 to 10%, depending on the desired result. In baked sweet goods and leavened cakes (like wedding or other special occasion cakes), butter is the fat more commonly used (substitutable with oil if needed) in higher quantities: from 20 to 40%.	Extra virgin olive oil, sunflower oil, coconut oil, butter, lard, almond cream, sesame cream (tahini).
Salt	Salt not only gives flavor to our bread, it also acts on the fermentation process by contributing to a dough's elasticity and structure, improving consistency and the formation of glutens. Of course, salt should be used sparingly, limited to about 2% with respect to the amount of flour. Moreover, being an enemy of yeasts and bacteria, salt should never come into direct contact with a sourdough starter. Add it halfway through the kneading, perhaps dissolved in a small amount of water.	Whole sea salt, other special salts such as: Guérande salt, Maldon salt, pink Himalayan salt.
Water	As noted in the dedicated paragraph, water is a fundamental element in the preparation of bread dough. The hydration percentage actually influences the final result in a considerable way. Try to choose a light water with low residue levels and, wherever possible, free of chlorine and calcium. Tap water is just fine, perhaps decanted or boiled before being used, otherwise run through a water filter.	

Type of ingredient	Effect on dough and bread	Examples
Milk	Milk and its derivatives (yogurt, kefir, buttermilk, etc.) are usually used in the preparation of leavened cakes and other sweets in place of water, either completely or partially. These ingredients make doughs softer as well as render flavors sweeter and slightly more acidic.	Milk, yogurt, kefir, buttermilk, etc.
Eggs	Fundamental in classics like wedding and other special occasion cakes, eggs enhance the flavor and nutritional components of a dough. They improve the look (fluffier texture, golden color) and act on the structure of the dough itself to increase elasticity and storing duration.	
Other liquids	In place of water, other liquids can be used, especially when you want more complex and interesting flavor and aroma in the final product. Vegetable-based drinks (rice, soy, oat, etc.) can also replace the cow's milk, if needed.	Fruit juices, beer, cider, vegetable juices, cooking liquids, infusions and herbal teas, vegetable-based drinks, coconut milk.
Spices and aromatic herbs, flakes and puffed grains, oily seeds, dried and dehydrated fruits	To enrich and decorate our breads, we have dozens of ingredients to choose from. These can have a strictly decorative purpose, or influence flavor and consistency. Oily seeds and dried or dehydrated fruits bring precious nutritional components to our bread, and they can help to limit additional fats or sweeteners in dough.	*Spices and aromatic herbs:* cinnamon, cardamom, cloves, coriander, cumin, curry, chives, dill, fennel, nutmeg, oregano, paprika, pepper, rosemary, vanilla, saffron, ginger, etc. *Flakes and puffed cereals:* oat flakes, puffed spelt, puffed millet, puffed rice, etc. *Oily seeds:* sesame, flax, sunflower, poppy, pumpkin, etc. *Dried fruits:* almonds, hazelnuts, walnuts, pistachios, pine nuts, pecans, macadamia nuts, peanut, cashews, etc. *Dehydrated fruit:* raisins, figs, apricots, plums, dates, etc.

And let's not forget cheeses, cured meats and sausages, fresh fruit, meat and vegetables: every chance to use up leftover items in the fridge or pantry will also lend a creative touch to breads!

MIXERS AND BREAD MACHINES: TECHNOLOGICAL MARVELS?

In recent years, interest in home breadmaking has increased exponentially, for many reasons: a desire for self-sufficiency and return to traditional family customs, better bread for oneself and one's family, and a quest for ingredients and characteristics (nutritional and flavorful) difficult to find in commercially baked goods.

A small amount of credit, if you will, is due to technology and the arrival of various types of affordable bread mixers and the even more widely used bread machines.
Even to those familiar with the magic of kneading by hand and those according to whom the best results are obtained through creating a symbiosis between dough and our hands (given the bacteria present on them), these tools are a considerable help to the budding baker.

Bread machines are essentially designed to cover the entire breadmaking process, from forming the dough to baking. Most of these appliances are equipped with fixed functions not easily modifiable, designed and standardized with the leavening times and temperatures for baker's yeast in mind.
As such, these machines are less useful when it comes to sourdough, except for perhaps the kneading phases, yet even here are not ideal given the smaller size of the mixing bowl.

Even household bread mixers are imperfect machines, according to professional bakers, but when used correctly they can provide excellent support in both simple tasks (even just for feeding) and more complex ones (such as "stretching" the dough of a *panettone* cake, for instance).
Like all machines, they cannot substitute for the human eye or experience. It's important to listen to, touch, and taste our starter dough so we know just when to act, whether it be the moment to start or stop a process, or to add more or less of a certain ingredient.
As mentioned prior, some models on today's market are moderately reliable. As a general rule, it's a good idea to choose one according to your own personal taste and needs, keeping in mind that they all are able to knead in a fairly satisfactory manner.

LEAVENING TIMES AND TEMPERATURES

Precise indications on leavening times and baking temperatures are hard to pinpoint. In the same way that no two starters or flours are alike, the many variables that influence a dough and its rising and baking methods make it difficult to provide universal or standardized instructions.

Firstly, let's look at room temperature.
The closer the leavening temperature gets to 26-30°C (79-86°F), the greater the activity and vitality of the yeasts and bacteria present in a dough.
With winter's typically lower temperatures (unless you have a proofing box), bread leavening slows down significantly. Temperatures higher than 35°C (95°F), whether natural or forced, will shorten fermentation times, but at the same time can cause defects in crust color and crumb development. More seriously, it can affect the digestibility of the final product.
In fact, bacteria and yeasts have an ideal temperature range in which they live and work best: where possible, we should try to respect this natural range, without resorting to temperatures too low (for example with forced leavening in the refrigerator) or too high.
Moreover, different families of microorganisms present in dough behave best at different temperatures: lower temperatures will encourage the yeasts to act, while higher temperatures favor lactic acid bacteria, resulting in different consistencies and tastes.

Nearly all the recipes in this book have been designed with a presumed constant internal room temperature of 22-24°C (72-75°F) in mind.

It's up to each individual home baker to adapt the indicated rising times to conditions like temperature and humidity at any given moment.

There's no need for tricky arithmetic and calculations here—just rely on your own sense and fine-tuned experience: in fact, a quick visual and tactile evaluation of your dough will be enough to understand where it is in the leavening phase.

Generally speaking, assuming you are using a mature and healthy sourdough starter, we can state the following:

Room temperature	Duration of the first rise	Second rise (after shaping)
16-22°C (61-71°F)	6-8 hours	2 hours
23-28°C (73.5-82.4 °F)	5-6 hours	1-2 hours
29°C (84°F) and higher	3-5 hours	0,5-1 hours

That said, leavening times are also influenced by the following:
- the type of bread or baked good desired
- room temperatures and humidity levels
- the kind of flour used (flours richer in glutens can sustain longer leavening periods)
- the health and quantity of the sourdough starter used (the stronger and more active the starter, the shorter the rising time will be)

FOLDING

Folding might seem at first an incomprehensible or useless act, but it's actually essential to good bread expansion during baking and it also helps reduce defects (see *Understanding and Addressing Problems* on page 33).

Done after the first rise, folding strengthens the gluten structure and encourages growth in the final rising phase when the dough has been shaped and left to rest before baking.

Without folding, the gluten structure will be weak and fragile, the dough will tend to over-leaven, and the bread is less likely to expand during baking and will probably result in an irregular and defective crumb.

The two most common types of bread folds are known as the "book" (or "envelope") fold and the "clock" fold.

Book folding is done by turning the risen dough out onto a floured cutting board. Lightly flatten the dough with your hands and form a rectangle, then fold one side over the other, overlapping about ⅔ of the shape. Next, fold the other side to overlap the first, closing it to form a smaller rectangle.

Now turn the dough 90° to the right and repeat the fold as outlined above.

You will have a small rectangle of layered folds, which you will let rest for a few minutes before shaping the dough.

Clock folding is perhaps less known, but it gives excellent results in terms of bread height during baking and quality of the crumb. As with book folding, start by turning out the dough onto a floured work surface. Lightly flatten the dough and form a circle. Pick up the dough from a point on the edge with your hands. Stretch the dough outwards from the center, then fold it back towards the center. Next, take the corner formed at the right side and continue in the same manner, turning a couple times counter-clockwise. When this is done, turn the ball over and let rest for a few minutes before proceeding with the shaping of the loaves.

BAGUETTE

DIVIDING AND SHAPING DOUGH

The final step before baking our bread is shaping the loaves.

The most frequently used shapes in both home and professional baking are round loaves and long loaves: simple and easy to make, especially for larger breads.

Every region in Italy has its own traditional bread shapes, from the hard-crusted bread of the Padana plains to the marvellous decorated breads of Sardinia. These complex shapes reflect a skill and experience on par with that of professional bakers.

Loaf tins are an easy and useful option for home. While they may not yield loaves that are particularly exciting to behold, they are perfect for those softer breads for slicing and toasting.

Moving beyond loaf shapes, countless other shapes exist for bakery products. From focaccia and pizza to breadsticks and crackers, the possibilities for adapting shapes to our needs and our imagination are endless, as reflected in the many recipes included in this book.

Images of some of the more classic bread shapes follow.

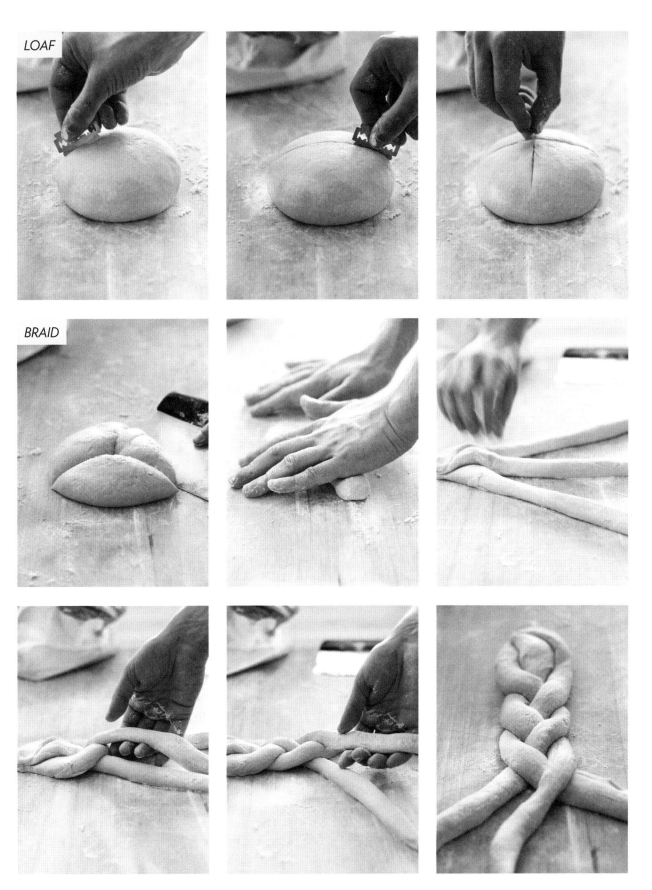

LOAF

BRAID

BAKING: THE OVEN CURES (ALMOST) ALL DEFECTS

Baking is clearly fundamental in making good bread, and when done right can help disguise or eliminate altogether any defects that occurred during leavening so you still achieve a good loaf. In turn, sloppy attention during baking (incorrect times or temperatures) can undo the hours of work you put into rising and shaping.

As is always the case, unequivocal cooking times and methods cannot be relied on given the many variables involved: the bread shape and size, the dough's hydration level, the type of oven used and maximum temperatures it can reach (not to mention how reliable one's thermostat is), the oven's internal humidity, and so on.

Every recipe in this book contains the most reliable cooking times and temperatures possible, but ultimately it is experience that will lead to the best results.

Keep these basic concepts in mind, generally:
- baking times are in direct relation to the size of the bread: larger breads require longer baking times;
- taller bread shapes will require baking times longer than those for more "flattened" shapes: a traditional loaf will bake longer than a pizza or focaccia, for instance;
- the higher a dough's hydration, the shorter the baking time will be;
- the more leavened the dough, and the more bubbly after shaping and rising, the shorter the baking time will be;
- the higher the oven's internal humidity (placing a pot of boiling water inside, for example), the faster the bread will bake.

Creating oven spring with heat

Almost all recipes advise placing bread in an oven that has been heated to its maximum temperature (usually 250°C/482°F), which is then lowered after around ten minutes to 200°C/392°F.

This initial "shock" of heat contributes to what's sometimes called oven spring. It's an important phase in a bread's final quality, helping to form good alveolation (crumb) and a nice crust. It's also during this phase in the overall bread-baking process that a bread will develop its maximum volume and size.

Never open the oven during these first few minutes, as doing so could cause the bread to collapse.

Steam in baking

Steam is at once a home baker's friend and enemy. Particularly in the first moments of baking, steam will improve the appearance of bread, but it is rather difficult to create this effect in domestic baking conditions.

Almost all breads, with the exception of rustic types such as those found in southern Italy, will require the use of steam during baking.

Steam achieves following:
- results in a glossier, thinner, crispier crust, as well as a softer, spongy crumb;
- speeds up cooking times;
- improves crust development during baking, reducing the risk of surface cracks and tears.

Ways to create steam in your own oven:
- just before placing the dough in the oven, set a small pot of boiling water inside, which will continue to boil and let off steam;
- while preheating, arrange an empty baking tray at the bottom of the oven and fill it with a few centimeters of water; this will heat up and form steam during baking;
- place an empty baking sheet in the oven; at the moment you put your dough in, place a few ice cubes on the tray;

The role of residual humidity in the oven during baking is very important. Unless otherwise instructed, wherever possible use your oven's static setting rather than ventilated, as the latter tends to dry out bread.

Baking stones

More and more people of late are using baking stones to obtain the best bread possible. Several types are available on the market today, all more or less based on the same basic principles.

A baking stone disperses heat more slowly, meaning that breads baked directly on the surface will benefit from uniform temperatures, usually higher than those possible without the stone.

An additional benefit of baking stones is that you can place the dough directly on a preheated surface (unlike with a baking tray, which will be at the same room temperature as the bread dough). This increases the bread's volume and helps the crumb structure.

Newer ovens, however, have fast preheating times, and can reach desired temperatures very quickly. In these cases, a baking stone can be rendered less useful or even counterproductive: stone disperses heat more slowly, so the risk here is that the dough starts to bake on a surface that is less hot than the internal oven temperature.

PIZZA BAKING

Pizza represents one of the greatest challenges to home bakers.

In professional wood-fired ovens of the kind found at pizzerias, pizza is baked at temperatures above 300-350° C/572-662° F). Obviously, recreating such conditions in one's home oven isn't realistic, but with some minor adjustments, good results can be obtained all the same.

The oven temperature must be set to the highest possible (250° C / 482° F or higher). Roll the dough out onto the baking tray and let rest for at least one hour before placing in the oven, on the lowest rack. Top the pizza with ingredients less susceptible to burning, such as tomato, but not mozzarella or other cheeses. When the pizza is almost done, then top it with other ingredients and return to the top rack of the oven, set to the grill function, and bake for a few more minutes to cook the just-added ingredients and melt the cheese.

DEFECTS: UNDERSTANDING AND ADDRESSING PROBLEMS

Leaving bad luck or the unexpected aside, the first loaves made with your new sourdough starter will likely have some minor flaws. But rest assured: homemade sourdough bread has never harmed anyone, and given its nutritional value and digestibility, it is almost always better than an industrially made bread found in supermarkets.

One thing is certain. At this early phase, you will probably end up with breads that are not as tall as you would like, with poor alveolation, and a sour flavor and aroma.

Have no fear. With a few tricks, an increasingly ripe starter, and growing experience on your part, you will learn to recognize, understand, and resolve your bread's defects.

Below is a list of the most common defects and their likely causes.

Bread is too sour	• the starter is not ripe • the rising time is too long • the rising temperature is too high • the flours used are too weak • the flours used are whole grain • there's too much starter in the dough
Bread is not tall enough	• the dough was not worked enough or was handled poorly before baking • the dough was not folded, or folded incorrectly

Bread is not tall enough	• the dough was over-leavened • the dough was not leavened enough • the oven temperature was too low • the oven temperature was too high • the flours used are too weak • too much salt was added to the dough • the dough was too hydrated
Defective alveolation (the best alveolation is comprised of small, uniformly distributed air bubbles. A bread with large, unevenly distributed bubbles may be impressive to see, but these are a sign of defective bread)	• the rising temperature is too high • the dough was not worked enough or was handled poorly before baking • the dough was not folded, or folded incorrectly • the dough was over-leavened • the salt was not mixed into the dough correctly
Pale crust with no crunch	• the oven temperature was too low • "old" flours were used • not enough salt was added

As you can see, some defects are caused by different and even contrary errors (a bread that fails to grow tall for instance can be due to an overly leavened dough or one that is not leavened enough), suggesting again that only experience and continuous practice can provide us with the ability to recognize our mistakes.

Especially in the beginning, taking notes on the dough, the doses of ingredients, and the methods carried out will surely help to better analyze defects and better understand the solutions available for future breadmaking.

STORING AND FREEZING BREAD

One of the advantages of sourdough bread is that it preserves well: it can keep for more than a week (but only if you don't eat it all first, of course!).

However, pay attention to your choice of ingredients and baking methods, taking some essential yet simple precautions to ensure that after all the work you've put into your bread, it is stored correctly. Incorrect storage methods can make bread go stale very quickly or encourage mold.

Once removed from the oven, let bread cool completely at room temperature and allow it to lose all its residual moisture (this could mean overnight). Wrap it in a cloth or a special kind of wrapping made for breads and place in paper bag (reusing those from prior purchases at the bakery is perfectly fine). Store in a dry place, away from humidity and direct sunlight.

To prolong the preservation time, close the wrapped bread tightly in a plastic bag to impede any residual moisture.

For even longer storing periods, freeze bread either whole in loaves (or smaller shapes) or sliced.

Wait a couple of days before freezing bread, however, during which time it should be stored as outlined above, given the presence of residual moisture in freshly baked bread. Residual water in bread that is frozen immediately will form ice micro-crystals harmful to the bread's structure, its flavor, and its digestibility.

SOURDOUGH STARTER VS. BAKER'S YEAST

Let's set aside baking powders for the moment (also called, in a somewhat misleading way in Italy, chemical yeasts, but in English known by the more correct term baking powder), as these are not yeasts at all but rather substances that expand the volume of doughs, breads and cakes due to a simple chemical reaction, not fermentation.

Compressed yeast, commonly called baker's yeast or brewer's yeast (given that at one time it was produced as a by-product of beer fermentation), is certainly the most widespread yeast used in homemade, artisan, or professional baking.

It comes in two forms: in fresh cakes or in dehydrated packages. These are the same type of product, both "raised" on molasses substrates, reduced to a cream, and then pressed into a cake shape or freeze-dried and packaged.

They both contain the same organism, a fungus called *Saccharomyces cerevisiae*, which during fermentation transforms sugars and starches into carbon dioxide (bubbles) and alcohol.

Basically, the presence of yeast makes doughs ferment, rise and become soft breads with good alveolation.

Unlike sourdough, a fermented dough in which dozens of families of lactic bacteria and different yeasts live, compressed yeasts can achieve leavening in much shorter periods of time (as short as an hour or less)—but at the expense of digestibility and flavor complexity. This is made possible by microorganisms perfectly adapted to fast fermentation, to produce products quickly and easily.

Moreover, breads produced with compressed yeast have very low acidity and less humidity than sourdough breads, and so they tend to dry out and become stale much quicker. In fact, while bread made with sourdough can keep for more than a week (again, on the condition you don't eat it all first!), breads made with baker's yeast will turn dry and hard after just a day.

From a strictly nutritional perspective, sourdough breads are much more digestible, since the microflora present in the dough are complex, composed of various types of yeasts and bacteria that work in close synergy with one another to metabolize the dough's contents, providing a kind of pre-digestion on our behalf.

DRIED SOURDOUGH STARTERS

As previously noted in the section dedicated to storing and keeping sourdough, the process of dehydrating or freeze-drying will damage yeasts and bacteria significantly, even killing off some of them. In the fast and invasive methods used in industrial or semi-industrial baking, the natural biodiversity present in a sourdough starter is put to a hard test.

Nearly all of the dried sourdough starters sold in commercial or even organic supermarkets do not actually work. Better said, they do not work as complete substitutes for an active and ripe sourdough starter. When you take a look at the list of ingredients on these products, in almost all cases a small amount of baker's yeast is included—in fact, the true creator of the fermentation here. In the few cases where baker's yeast is not present, you'll find all the same a note—usually in a barely visible or correct way—to add baker's yeast to your recipe.

Thus, in these cases, dried sourdough does not play a role in fermentation as much as it simply creates flavor characteristics in the dough. And it's not by chance that in professional and industrial baking, dried sourdough is used to improve breads.

CONVERTING RECIPES FROM BAKER'S YEAST TO SOURDOUGH

Sourdough, as mentioned several times, is a live dough, rich in biodiversity and never the same from one to the next as it can mutate very easily over time, depending on variables such as temperature, humidity, type of flour, the hands that knead it, and so on. Providing a clear and unequivocal formula, therefore, with regard to the relationship between sourdough and compressed yeasts is not at all easy.

Recreating and indeed improving any recipe by using sourdough instead of compressed yeast is certainly possible. It requires a bit more attention and love, but the results will not disappoint.

Depending on the recipe, a certain amount of yeast will be needed, the percentage of which being determined by the method used, whether direct or indirect (with the use of a pre-ferment).

Additionally, the health of the starter along with its hydration level will naturally influence the amount used in the dough.

If we take into account the recommended average amounts published in commercially marketed packets of baker's yeast (whether fresh cakes or freeze-dried packets) together with an average healthy sourdough starter (of which typically 20-30% is used in the dough), we can propose the following:

Amount of flour	Amount of cake yeast	Amount of freeze-dried yeast	Sourdough starter
500 g (17.6 oz)	25 g (.9 oz)	7 g (.25 oz)	100-150 g (3.5-5.3 oz)

In percentages, this comes to:

Amount of flour	Amount of cake yeast	Amount of freeze-dried yeast	Sourdough starter
100%	5%	1,4%	20-30%

Those for whom a formula is helpful can follow this:

Amount of sourdough starter = (30 x recommended amount of cake yeast) / 5

For example, if the recipe calls for 15 g of baker's yeast, we will add
30 x 15 / 5 = 90 g of sourdough starter.

These amounts are only indicative, however, to provide the basis for creating your own recipe.

EVERYDAY BREADS

Simple, hearty breads, the kind perfect for dipping in leftover bits
of sauce on your plate, that last spoonful of jam, or a few slices
of prosciutto. These are the rustic-looking breads of every day,
substantial yet soft on the inside.

WHOLE WHEAT BAGUETTES À L'ITALIENNE (AUTOLYZE METHOD)

Forget those pre-cooked and frozen baguettes bought at the store that turn chewy two hours after being purchased. These baguettes will fill your home with the essence of a French boulangerie with their whole-grain fragrance, crunch, and softness. Taste them fresh out of the oven (after cooling, of course)!

FOR TWO BAGUETTES ABOUT **250** G
(9 OZ) EACH

THE FIRST DOUGH (AUTOLYZE)
200 g (1 & ⅔ cup) whole wheat flour
100 ml (½ cup) water
A pinch of salt

MAIN DOUGH
All of the first dough
100 g (3.5 oz) of fed starter
50 ml (¼ cup) water
A pinch of salt

Make the first dough by mixing the flour with the water and salt, kneading for about 10 minutes. Let rest in a covered bowl at room temperature for 8-12 hours. Add the remaining ingredients to the prepared mixture: the starter, water, and a pinch of salt.

Knead well (which might be a little challenging at first) until a well-hydrated loaf forms. Let rise in a covered bowl for about 1 hour.

Turn the dough out onto a floured work surface. Do a cycle of folds and form two baguette shapes. Place them on a baking sheet covered with baking paper, folding the paper to create vertical walls to sustain the dough (otherwise they might collapse, given the hydration level).

Cover and let rest for about 2 hours.

Meanwhile bring 500 ml (2 cups) water to the boil in a small steel pot. Heat the oven to 250°C/480°F. Just before transferring to the oven, score the surface of the loaves diagonally with a very sharp knife. Place the pot of water in the oven and then the baguettes. Bake for 25-30 minutes.

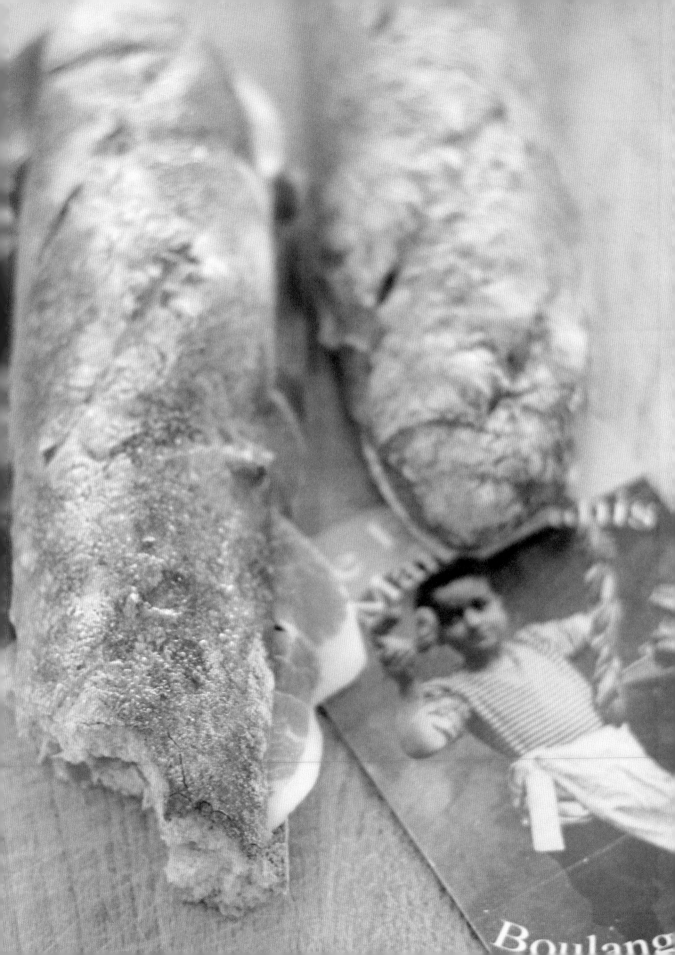

OLIVE OIL *CROCETTINE*

As a child, I used to walk with my grandmother to the neighborhood bakery every morning. There we would buy the bread known as baffo bolognese *along with warm, cross-shaped rolls called* crocettine *(something like "little crosses"), just out of the oven to accompany us on the way home. This version calls for extra virgin olive oil instead of lard, but it's just as tasty and flaky as the original. This was my favorite childhood snack.*

FOR ABOUT **20** PIECES

200 g (7 oz) of fed starter
1 kg (8 cups) organic type '0' flour (or all-purpose)
400 ml (1 & ⅔ cups) water
100 ml (⅓ cup) extra virgin olive oil
3 tsp salt

Dissolve the fed starter in the water. Mix thoroughly and begin adding the flour slowly, kneading with your hands or with a wooden spoon.

When you have added half the flour, add the salt and olive oil to the dough and continue kneading until all the other ingredients are added.

This is a hard, low hydration dough, so it could be a bit tricky to work by hand. If so, use a rolling pin or wooden spoon to knead and work the dough.

Cover and let rest in a bowl for about 6 hours, until doubled in volume.

Transfer the dough to a work surface and form small loaves weighing about 100 g (3.5 oz) each.

Roll each ball out to tubes 20 cm (8 in) long and 3 cm (1.2 in) in diameter.

Next flatten them out with the rolling pin to form rectangular strips measuring about 20 x 5 cm (8 x 2 in) by .5 cm (.2 in).

Holding the dough out in front of you and using your right hand, from the top begin rolling and unrolling, pressing with the palm of your hand and fingers while unrolling, and then rolling again but without pressing. Continue until you have rolled half of the strip and have a long, thin roll.

Turn the dough and continue in the same manner described above. You should have two long, thin rolls made from the strips, bound together by a small piece of dough.

Now rotate the right one twice so that a sort of knot is formed in the middle.

Place on the work surface and lightly press at the center of the knot to affix the two rolls.

Continue in this manner until you have 20 *crocettine*.

Arrange the shapes on a baking sheet lined with baking paper and let rise for a couple of hours.

Bake in a preheated oven (with a small pot of boiling water inside) for about 30 minutes at 180°C/355°F.

PUFFED QUINOA AND POPPY SEED LOAF

*This tasty bread calls for somewhat unusual ingredients and is sure to surprise
you with its consistency, toasted aroma, and an at-once crunchy and soft texture.
Try this one for breakfast, or surprise your friends at dinner time!*

FOR 1 LOAF

150 g (5.3 oz) of fed starter
500 g (4 cups) all-purpose wheat flour
250 ml (1 cup) water
100 g (3.5 oz) puffed quinoa
50 g (6 tbsp) poppy seeds
2 tsp salt

Combine the starter with the water and dissolve well. Add half of the flour and
begin to knead.
Add the puffed quinoa, poppy seeds, salt and remaining flour, continuing to work
until a smooth, uniform mixture forms.
Let rise in a covered bowl for 5-6 hours.
Fold the dough and form a loaf shape. Let rest covered on a baking sheet lined with
baking paper for another two hours.
Bake in an oven preheated to 250°C/480°F for 10 minutes, then lower the
temperature to 200°C/390°F and continue baking for another 30 minutes.

GLUTEN-FREE CORN AND RICE FLOUR ROLLS

Breadmaking entails constant experimentation, including testing out gluten-free flours.
These small rolls bring together the color of corn, the lightness of rice, and
the heartiness of lupin beans. Working gluten-free dough is not easy, but
the flavor of these small round rolls make them worth the effort.

FOR ABOUT **10** PIECES

100 g (3.5 oz) of fed starter
150 g (⅔ cup) rice flour
150 g (¾ cup) corn flour
100 g (¾ cup) tapioca flour
100 g (1 cup) lupin bean flour
   (or chickpea flour)
250 ml (1 cup) water
Whites of 1 egg
2 tsp salt

Combine the starter and water until completely dissolved.
Add the flours and begin to work the dough with your hands or with a spoon.
Shortly after add the egg whites and salt.
Mix thoroughly and carefully to combine all ingredients as best you can. This gluten-free dough will naturally be crumbly, grainy, and difficult to work.
Next, flour your hands well and form ten small roll shapes. Let them rest on a baking sheet covered with baking paper for at least 6-7 hours.
Cover the baking sheet with a piece of aluminum foil and bake at 180°C/355 °F for about 30 minutes. Remove the foil and continue baking for another 20 minutes.

BARLEY FLOUR *FRISE*

A tribute to traditional friselle *from the Puglia region, these ring-shaped breads evoke the sun and earth with their aroma, and require nothing more than a quality extra virgin olive oil (preferably a flavorful variety), sea salt and a few crushed, ripe cherry tomatoes.*

FOR ABOUT **20** PIECES

150 g (5.3 oz) of fed starter
200 g (1 & ⅓ cups) whole grain
   barley flour
100 g (⅔ cup) durum wheat semolina
   flour
180 ml (just under ¾ cup) water
2 tsp salt

Dissolve the starter in the water, add the flours and begin to combine. Shortly after, add the salt and work with your hands until a smooth, uniform mixture forms. Transfer the dough to a bowl, cover and let rise for 5-6 hours.

Fold the dough. Divide into 10 loaves weighing about 50 g (1.75 oz) each. With each piece of dough, form a long loaf measuring 1 cm (.4 in) in diameter. Close up the pieces again to form a ring shape and transfer to a baking sheet lined with baking paper.

Let rise again for 2-3 hours.

Meanwhile, heat the oven to 220°C/430°F and bake the loaves for 20 minutes. Remove from the oven and slice in half while still warm. Place all the sliced halves back on the baking sheet with the insides facing up. Return to the oven and bake for another 30 minutes at 180°C/355°F. Remove from the oven and let cool completely.

RYE AND SPELT *PAARL*

Hailing from Italy's Alto Adige region, the specialty bread known as paarl *(whose name means "couple" in area dialect) is the perfect snack for after a lovely walk in the mountains. They're typically served lightly toasted and topped with speck, mustard, alpeggio cheeses (from mountain pasture herds), and pickles, alongside a cold beer. This bread evokes the sights and sounds of the Alps, clear breezes, and cows grazing under a bright blue sky.*

FOR **3** *PAARL*

150 g (5.3 oz) of fed starter
350 g (2 & ¾ cups) rye flour
150 g (1 & ½ cups) white spelt flour
400 ml (1 & ⅔ cups) water
3 tsp salt
1 tsp mixed herbs for rye breads
    (caraway, fenugreek, fennel)

Dissolve the starter in the water and add the rest of the ingredients (leaving the salt for last). Knead and work the dough thoroughly. Once the dough has formed, let rest in a bowl covered with a tea towel for about 4 hours.

Transfer the dough to a well-floured work surface. Divide and form short, round loaves weighing about 200 g (7 oz) each. Arrange the "couples" next to each other on a baking sheet covered with baking paper. The idea is that the two loaves will merge together as they rise again. Cover with a tea towel and let rest for a couple hours more.

Preheat the oven to 200°C/390°F and bake for about 30 minutes.

DURUM WHEAT *MAFALDINE*

For a half-Sicilian like myself, sesame is not just a garnish, but rather a fundamental ingredient in every kind of bread. Added to dough and sprinkled on top of a loaf, sesame seeds lend color, flavor, and warm, delicious aromas to bread. The Sicilian bread featured here known as mafalda *is crunchy on the outside and soft inside, and it brings all the golden colors of Sicily's durum wheat fields at your table.*

FOR 4 PIECES

150 g (5.3 oz) of fed starter
400 g (2 & ¼ cups) durum wheat
   semolina flour
250 ml (1 cup) water
1 tsp sesame seeds
1 tsp salt

TO DECORATE

2 tsp sesame seeds

Dissolve the starter in the water. Add the flour and 1 teaspoon of the sesame seeds. Begin to knead.

Halfway through kneading, add the salt. Continue working until an elastic dough forms.

Let rise at room temperature in a covered bowl for 4-5 hours, until doubled in volume.

Transfer the dough to a work surface and do a cycle of folds. Divide into 4 loaves weighing 200 g each (7 oz), and shape each into a long, thin loaf.

Fold each onto to itself to form a snake shape, until you reach ⅔ of the each piece's length. Lift this last uncoiled bit and drape it lengthwise over the snake-shaped portion of the loaf.

Transfer the loaves to a baking sheet covering with baking paper, cover and let rise for a couple hours.

Just before baking, brush the surfaces with a small amount of water and dust generously with sesame seeds. Bake at 200°C/390°F for about 20-25 minutes.

This simple bread is full of the rustic flavor of unrefined grain. Choose a whole-grain, stone-ground, organic flour. Your bread, and your body, will thank you.

WHOLE GRAIN OAT
BRAN LOAF

When I think of the city of Altamura in Italy's Puglia region, old historic bakeries and the hypogea subterranean structures always come to mind. This city's historic center features centuries-old wood-fired ovens, where families of bakers have always worked the night through to produce hundreds of loaves at a time. Here, the simple yet swift kneading of bread is almost a tribal ritual. The smells from those places will always live in my head and in my heart as the true aroma of bread.

ALTAMURA BREAD

With its golden color and intense aroma, this bread will win you over with every slice, as it did with me. Its flavor is rich but not overly so, and soon it will be the bread you always crave at breakfast—or lunch, or dinner, or a midnight snack...

SPELT AND CHICKPEA FLOUR BREAD

WHOLE GRAIN OAT BRAN LOAF

FOR 1 LOAF

100 g (3.5 oz) of fed starter

350 g (2 & ¾ cups) soft whole
   wheat flour

300 ml (1 & ¼ cups) water

150 g (1 & ⅔ cups) oat bran

1 tsp salt

Dissolve the starter in the water and add the flour and oat bran.

Begin kneading. Add the salt and continue working until a smooth, consistent dough forms.

Let rise in a bowl at room temperature for about 5 hours, until doubled in volume.

Next, transfer the dough to a floured work surface. Do a cycle of folds and form a long loaf.

Moisten the surface of the loaf and dust it with some of the oat bran.

Cover with a tea towel and let rise again for 1 hour. Bake in an oven preheated to 250°C/480°F for the first 10 minutes, and for another 20 minutes at 200°C/390°F (about 30 minutes total).

ALTAMURA BREAD

FOR 1 LOAF

150 g (5.3 oz) of fed starter

500 g (3 cups) durum wheat semolina
   flour (if possible, the Senatore
   Cappelli variety)

300 ml (1 & ¼ cups) water

2 tsp salt

Dissolve the starter in the water. Add the flour and begin to knead.

Shortly after, add the salt and continue working until the dough is elastic, moist, and smooth.

Cover and let rest in a bowl for 5-6 hours at room temperature.

Work the dough again on a floured surface. Do a cycle of clock folds as you shape into a round loaf by lifting the dough on one side and folding it back towards the center. Transfer the loaf to a baking sheet covered with baking paper and cover.

Let rise another 2 hours circa. Bake in an oven preheated to 250°C/480°F for 15 minutes. Lower the temperature to 200°C/390°F and continue baking for another 30-35 minutes.

SPELT AND CHICKPEA FLOUR BREAD

FOR 1 LOAF

150 g (5.3 oz) of fed starter

450 g (4 & ½ cups) spelt flour

150 g (1 & ⅔ cups) chickpea flour

250 ml (1 cup) water

1 tsp salt

Combine the chickpea flour with 150 ml (⅔ cup) of water in a bowl. Let rest at room temperature for about two hours.

After two hours, dissolve the starter with 100 ml (½ cup) of water. Add the spelt flour, the chickpea flour dough made prior, and lastly the salt.

Work the dough until you have a smooth, uniform loaf. Place in a bowl. Cover and let rest at room temperature for about 5 hours.

Once risen, transfer the loaf to a work surface and do a cycle of clock folds, forming a loaf again. Let rise for another hour circa. Score the surface with a very sharp knife.

Lightly flour and bake for 40 minutes: the first 10 minutes at 250°C/480°F and the remaining 30 minutes at 180°C/355°F.

ICELANDIC BREAD

This recipes comes all the way from Iceland—where, like other parts of Northern Europe, barley is common—specifically from a biodynamic farmer who gave me a package of whole-grain, stone-ground barley flour to use for making bread. I dedicate this loaf to him, to his smile, to his hands roughened by the cold, and to his work to protect and preserve biodiversity.

FOR 1 LOAF

100 g (3.5 oz) of fed starter
300 g (2 cups) whole barley flour
200 ml (¾ cup) water
100 g (3.5 oz) barley flakes
2 tsp salt

TO DECORATE
2 tsp barley flakes

Dissolve the starter in the water. Add the barley flour and begin to work the dough with your hands.

Shortly after, add the barley flakes and salt. Continue kneading until a uniform mixture forms.

Let rest in a covered bowl for about 6 hours at room temperature.

Once risen, turn the dough out onto a well-floured work surface. Shape the dough into a loaf and transfer to a bread tin lined with baking paper. Brush the surface with a small amount of water and sprinkle generously with the barley flakes.

Cover the loaf and let rise for another 2-3 hours. Bake in an oven preheated to 200°C/390°F for 35-40 minutes.

MULTI-GRAIN BREAD WITH PUFFED MILLET

In Anthroposophy, the characteristics of every grain are mirrored in those of a certain day of the week and planet. This recipe includes six of them in one bread, each a vital component rich in essential nutrients.

FOR 1 LOAF

150 g (5.3 oz) of fed starter
300 g (4 cups) all-purpose wheat flour
50 g (⅓ cup) whole grain rye flour
50 g (⅓ cup) whole grain barley flour
50 g (⅓ cup) whole grain rice flour
50 g (⅓ cup) whole grain oat flour
300 ml (1 & ¼ cups) water
30 g (1 & ½ cups) puffed millet
2 tsp salt

Dissolve the starter in the water. Add the flours and begin to knead.
When the dough is just about formed, add the salt and the puffed millet and knead until a smooth and consistent dough is formed.
Let rise in a covered bowl for 4-5 hours, until doubled in size.
Transfer the dough to a floured work surface. Do a cycle of clock folds and form a round loaf. Cover and let rest for about another two hours.
Score the surface with a sharp knife. Bake at 250°C/480°F for 10 minutes, then another 25 minutes at 200°C/390°F.

RUSTIC LOAF WITH SENATORE CAPPELLI DURUM WHEAT

I had the fortune to see a field of organic Senatore Cappelli durum wheat in the Murge region in Southern Italy, during an end-of-spring sunset. A light wind blew through the tall spikes of wheat, still green yet touched with golden reflections from the sun. The scene was like a ocean singing, and all the joy and festivity of that image lives on in this bread.

FOR 1 LOAF

100 g (3.5 oz) of fed starter
1 kg (5 & ¼ cups) durum wheat flour
  (Senatore Cappelli variety)
600 ml (2 & ½ cups) water
2 tsp salt

Dissolve the starter in the water and begin to add the flour, kneading well. When nearly all the flour has been mixed in, add the salt and continue working until a smooth, consistent dough forms.

Let rise in a covered bowl for 5-6 hours, until doubled in volume. Turn the dough out onto a floured surface and do a cycle of clock folds as you form a round loaf. Cover with a tea towel and let rise for a couple hours more.

Score and bake in an oven heated to 250°C/480°F for 10 minutes, then bake another 40-50 minutes at 200°C/390°F.

YEAST-FREE WHOLE GRAIN SPELT LOAF (WITH BACKFERMENT)

Have a look at the photo of this bread. This is a bread made without leavening. If you're as passionate as I am about the world of quality breadmaking, you simply must try this bread, which is leavened with only lactic acid bacteria.
The processing is laborious and longer than usual, requiring more attention to rising temperatures. But I can already imagine the satisfaction you will feel as you smile at a friend with yeast intolerance and give him or her this bread made with your own hands.

FOR 1 LOAF

FOR THE FIRST DOUGH

20 g (.7 oz) of backferment (or baking
    ferment; see below)
200 g (1 & ⅓ cups) whole barley flour
200 ml (¾ cup) warm water
    (35-40°C/95-104°F circa)

FOR THE SECOND DOUGH

Dough made previously
300 g (2 cups) whole barley flour
150 ml (⅔ cup) warm water
    (35-40°C/95-104°F circa)
1 tsp raisins, soaked in water
1 tsp salt

Dissolve the backferment in the warm water and add the flour. Combine well using a wooden spoon. Cover the bowl with a tea towel and let rest for about 12 hours at a temperature of 25-30°C/77-86°F. In winter use an oven that's been turned off but still warm inside.

Add the water, flour, raisins, and salt to the first dough and knead for at least 20 minutes. If the dough is too sticky, use a wooden spoon to help.

Cover and let rise for another 4-5 hours.

Transfer the leavened dough to a well-floured wooden block or work surface and form a loaf shape. Place inside a bread tin lined with baking paper. Let rest for another hour.

Cover the tin completely with a sheet of aluminum foil and bake at 180-200°C/355-390°F for 30 minutes. Remove the foil and continue baking at the same temperature for another 20-25 minutes.

BACKFERMENT AND BAKING WITH LACTIC ACID BACTERIA

Sourdough starter is rich in several strains of yeast and bacteria that influence fermentation and bread flavor in different ways. Among these, lactic bacteria carry out a slower, more delicate kind of fermentation (and require rising temps that are slightly higher and constant). They give bread a unique flavor, sweet and aromatic, with very little acidity. Moreover, with the growth of baker's yeast (Saccharomyces cerevisiae) intolerance, this ferment is an interesting option for making "yeast-free" breads. A backferment (or baking ferment) is a traditional, historical product developed at the beginning of the last century by Hubo Erbe, an exponent of the philosophic and bio-dynamic movement Anthroposophy. Originally based on the vital dualism of honey/salt, today backferment can be found in markets (usually organic food shops), packaged in sachets or in small jars.
In short, a backferment is strictly lactic acid based, and results in small, uniformly distributed alveoli (bubbles) and a characteristic slightly sweet aroma.

MULTI-GRAIN PUMPERNICKEL

Rich in fiber, this German rye bread is typically sliced into rectangle shapes and often used in preparing starters like savory canapes. The version here is softer, made from spelt flour and additional grains for diverse flavor and an almost crunchy consistency.

FOR 1 LOAF

70 g (2.5 oz) of fed starter
250 g (2 & ½ cups) white spelt flour
150 g (5-6 oz) mixed grains (oats,
   wheat, rye, brown rice, barley, spelt)
130 ml (just under ⅔ cup) water
20 g (1 tbsp) cane sugar molasses
1 tsp salt

Cook the various grains in water in a small pot, as if you were making a soup. Depending on the varieties used, this could take about an hour. Once cooked, drain and let cool.

Combine the starter with the water in a bowl. Add the molasses and the spelt flour. Begin to knead. Halfway through the kneading, add the salt and the cooked cereals, working the mixture well to thoroughly combine all the ingredients.

Cover the bowl with a tea towel and let rest for 4-5 hours at room temperature. Work the dough on a floured surface. Do a cycle of folds and form a small loaf. Transfer to a bread tin lined with baking paper.

Let rest for about another two hours. Preheat the oven to 180°C/355°F.

Cover the tin with a sheet of aluminum foil, leaving a little space for expansion during baking. Bake for 30 minutes, then remove the foil and continue baking for another 20 minutes.

WHOLE GRAIN ROLLS WITH WILD FENNEL

These fragrant rolls bring together wheat flour and aromatic herbs (in my case, those growing on my terrace) and go very well with flavorful cured meats and cold cuts.

FOR **7** PIECES

200 g (7 oz) of fed starter
350 g (2 & ¾ cups) all-purpose flour
350 g (2 & ¾ cups) whole wheat flour
350 ml (1 & ½ cups) water
50 ml (3 & ½ tbsp) extra virgin olive oil
1 tsp honey
1 tsp fennel seeds
1 tsp wild fennel pollen
1 tsp salt

Dissolve the starter in the water. Add the honey and the flours and begin to knead. Add the remaining ingredients and combine the mixture thoroughly until smooth. Transfer to a bowl and cover with a tea towel. Let rest for 5-6 hours at room temperature.

Transfer the dough to a floured work surface. Do a cycle of folds and let rest another hour. Then form seven small round rolls, weighing about 200 g (7 oz) each. Arrange the rolls on a baking sheet, cover and let rest for a couple hours more.

Score a cross design on the surfaces and bake in an oven preheated to 200°C/390°F for about 20 minutes.

DURUM WHEAT *SPACCATELLE* WITH TOASTED SUNFLOWER SEEDS

These small, sun-inspired rolls take their name from the Sicilian curved pasta spaccatelle. Pair them with something tasty of your choosing, and they're sure to have you longing for a relaxing picnic under the shade of a tree.

FOR **12** PIECES

250 g (8.8 oz) of fed starter
600 g (3 & ⅔ cups) durum wheat
   semolina flour
300 ml (1 & ½ cups) water
150 g (5.3 oz) sunflower seeds
2 tsp salt

Toast the sunflower seeds in a nonstick pan for a few minutes.
Dissolve the starter in the water, add the semolina flour, and begin to knead.
Continue to work the dough. Add the seeds and the salt.
Let rise in a covered bowl for 4-5 hours, until doubled in size.
Transfer the dough to a floured surface. Do a cycle of folds and form small ball shapes, each weighing about 100 g (3.5 oz).
Cover with a towel and let rest another two hours circa. Score them diagonally with a sharp knife. Bake for 10 minutes at 250°C/480°F for 10 minutes, then lower the heat to 200°C/390°F and bake for another 20 minutes.

EINKORN WHEAT LOAF

Einkorn wheat is one of the oldest grains ever cultivated, the ancestor of hard and soft grains we use today. Rustic, flavorful, fragrant, with an intense golden color, einkorn exudes the colors and aromas of wheat fields in August.

FOR 1 LOAF

150 g (5.3 oz) of fed starter
500 g (5 cups) einkorn wheat flour
250 ml (1 cup) water
2 tsp salt

TO DECORATE
2 tsp wheat bran

Dissolve the starter in the water and begin to add the einkorn flour, working the dough well with your hands. Add the salt and continue kneading until a uniform, smooth dough has formed.

Let rise in a covered bowl for 4-5 hours, until doubled in size.

Work the dough on a floured surface. Do a cycle of folds and form one loaf. Cover and let rest for another two hours on a baking sheet lined with baking paper.

Heat the oven to 250°C/480°F.

Brush the surface of the loaf with a bit of water and decorate with the bran. Score the loaf with a sharp knife in a wheat spike design (see photo).

Bake for 30-40 minutes: the first 10 minutes at 250°C/480°F and the remaining at 200°C/390°F.

TUSCAN DURUM WHEAT LOAF

Flour and water are the only ingredients you need to make bread. Here I've brought together different traditions—a Tuscan method and a Southern Italian flour—to create a bread that reflects the richness of each region.

FOR 1 LOAF

150 g (5.3 oz) of fed starter
500 g (3 & ⅔ cups) durum wheat
   semolina flour
260 ml (1 & ⅛ cups) water

Combine the starter and water until completely dissolved.
Add the flour, mixing thoroughly and kneading until a smooth, uniform, elastic dough forms.
Let rest in a covered bowl at room temperature for 4-5 hours.
Transfer the dough to a floured work surface. Do a cycle of book folds and shape into a loaf. Place on a baking sheet lined with baking paper.
Cover and let rise for another 3 hours circa. Flour the surface and bake for 15 minutes in an oven heated to 250°C/480°F. Lower the temperature to 200°C/390°F and continue baking for another 40 minutes.

SOFT SANDWICH BREAD (ASIAN STYLE)

I've never been a fan of sliced bread, the kind used for soft sandwiches known in Italy as tramezzini. *To me it lacks flavor and fragrance, and has a flimsy crumb. Then I tried this bread, which is soft yet very flavorful, a truly perfect match for an afternoon snack. Try it with a layer of homemade jam or chocolate cream.*

FOR **1** LOAF

FOR THE *THANG ZONG* STARTER (WATER ROUX)
20 g (2 & ½ tbsp) all-purpose flour
100 ml (½ cup) water

FOR THE DOUGH
Thang zong starter
100 g (3.5 oz) of fed sourdough starter
300 g (2 & ⅓ cups) all-purpose flour
150 ml (⅔ cup) water
30 g (1 oz) agave syrup
30 ml (2 & ¼ tbsp) sesame oil
1 tsp salt

A bread tin greased with oil or butter

Using a whisk, slowly combine the flour and water in a small pot until a batter forms. Heat the batter on the stove top and continue mixing until it reaches a temperature of 65°C/150°F.
Check the temperature using a small food thermometer. Lacking a thermometer, remove the batter from the heat as soon as it begins to thicken and turn translucent. Next cover the pot with cling wrap so the surface of the mixture does not dry out. Let cool.

Dissolve the sourdough starter in the water in a bowl. Add the starter just made, the flour, and the agave syrup. Begin to knead.
Halfway through the kneading add the salt and then the sesame oil and combine thoroughly. Cover and let rise at room temperature for 4-5 hours.
Turn the dough out onto a floured work surface. Do a cycle of book folds and then form a long loaf. Place the loaf in the tin previously greased. Let rise a couple hours more, until the loaf has just about reached the top of the tin. Bake at 200°C/390°F for about 40 minutes. Use a toothpick to check the readiness of the loaf.
Turn out of the tin and let cool completely before slicing.

NOTE: If you do not have a standard bread tin with a closing lid, you can use a loaf tin (such as those used for cakes). Place a layer of lightly greased baking paper on top and cover with a heavy oven-proof board. The dough will stop growing as it bakes when it reaches the top.

POTATO AND GARLIC *ZOCCOLETTI*

I love potato and garlic, even more so when the two ingredients are brought together.
In this recipe, the potato creates softness while the garlic lends a subtle yet unmistakable aroma.

FOR ABOUT **10** PIECES

150 g (5.3 oz) of fed starter
500 g (4 cups) all-purpose flour
200 ml (¾ cup) water
200 g (7 oz) floury potatoes
50 ml (3 & ½ tbsp) extra virgin olive oil
3 garlic cloves
2 tsp salt

Boil the potatoes. Mash them or process them with a food mill and let cool. Finely chop the garlic until it is almost a cream.

Dissolve the starter in the water, add the flour, and begin to knead.

Halfway through kneading add the remaining ingredients, including the garlic and salt, and continue kneading until a smooth and elastic dough forms.

Let rise at room temperature in a covered bowl for about 5 hours, until doubled in volume.

Do a cycle of clock folds on a floured work surface. Cover and let rest for another hour circa, then form small oval loaves (imagine a potato shape). Roll the shapes in flour. Transfer the loaves to a baking sheet lined with baking paper. Cover and let rest another two hours.

Bake in an oven preheated to 200°C/390°F for 10 minutes, then lower the temperature to 180°C/355°F and continue baking for another 15 minutes.

BREAKFAST AND SNACK BREADS

When the alarm clock rings, nothing helps us ease into the day like a good breakfast. Soft, fragrant, sweet morsels hiding a little surprise inside—these breads will make children happy and comfort adults at both breakfast and snack time.

COFFEE AND BANANA BREAD

This revised version of the classic American banana bread brings together the soft sweetness of banana and the incredibly rich, full flavor of coffee for delicious results.

FOR 1 LOAF

100 g (3.5 oz) of fed starter
350 g (2 & ¾ cups) all-purpose flour
150 ml (⅔ cup) water
100 g (½ cup) brown cane sugar
50 g (3 & ½ tbsp) butter
2 eggs
2 bananas
1 tbsp ground coffee
A pinch of salt

Dissolve the sourdough starter in the water until you have a smooth batter. Add the flour and work with your hands to obtain a uniform mixture.

Meanwhile, soften the butter at room temperature. Beat the eggs. Mash the bananas with a fork until creamy.

Combine all the remaining ingredients in the bowl, including the salt and the coffee, and begin to mix the dough.

This might be a bit challenging at the beginning, given that you are adding semi-liquid ingredients to an already formed mixture. Yet it's important to continue kneading carefully until a homogeneous mixture forms.

Let rise in a covered bowl for 5-6 hours.

Work the dough on a floured work surface. Do a cycle of book folds and shape into a loaf. Transfer to a plum cake loaf tin lined with baking paper. Let rise another 2-3 hours. Bake in an oven heated to 200°C/390°F for about one hour.

BOMBOLINI

These are mini versions of the celebrated Italian cream-filled pastries called bomboloni, *only without the cream filling, so good you'll enjoy them one after another. Try not to fight over them!*

FOR ABOUT **30** *BOMBOLINI*

100 g (3.5 oz) of fed starter
300 g (2 & ⅓ cups) all-purpose flour
70 ml (just over ¼ cup) milk
30 g (2 tbsp) butter, softened
1 egg
1 tsp brown sugar (2 for sweeter
   bombolini)
A pinch of salt
Seed oil for frying
2 tbsp brown sugar (or powdered sugar)
   to garnish

Dissolve the starter in the milk. Add the flour and combine.
Beat the egg and add to the mix along with the butter, sugar and salt. Knead until a soft dough forms. Cover with a tea towel and let rise for about 5 hours.
Roll out the dough on a flour work surface to about 1-cm thickness (.4 in).
Press out circles 3 cm in diameter (1.2 in) using a cookie cutter or glass.
Let rise again for another 2 hours, then fry in plenty of hot oil.
Drain the *bomboloni* from the oil and transfer to a paper towel to remove excess oil.
Dust with the brown sugar while still warm (or let them cool completely and dust generously with powdered sugar).

SPELT FLOUR *BUCHTELN*

Buchteln are my mother's favorite dessert, either alone or accompanied by warm vanilla cream. These sweet, soft buns from Italy's Alto Adige region are made by shaping small pieces, which are first separated and then put back together. Dusted with powdered sugar, and served either alone or accompanied by warm vanilla cream, they are perfect for sharing with family or friends as a snack after a walk—like a souvenir from a mountain holiday. A warm cup of coffee served alongside them is a must!

FOR 6 PIECES

100 g (3.5 oz) of fed starter
250 g (2 & ½ cups) white spelt flour
100 ml (⅓ cup) milk
25 g (1 & ¾ tbsp) butter, softened
35 g (¼ cup) brown sugar
1 egg
Zest of 1 lemon (grated)
A pinch of salt

FOR THE FILLING

100 g (3.5 oz) hazelnuts, finely chopped
100 ml (⅓ cup) milk
30 g (¼ cup) brown sugar
½ tsp vanilla powder

Melted butter for brushing

Dissolve the starter in the milk. Add the spelt flour a little at a time.
Shortly after, begin adding all the remaining ingredients a little at a time to the mixture. Work thoroughly until you have a well-combined dough.
Cover with a tea towel and let rise in a bowl for at least 6 hours, until doubled in volume.
In the meantime, make the filling. Place the chopped nuts, milk, sugar, and vanilla in a small pot and warm until it thickens. Remove from heat and let cool at room temperature.
When the dough has risen, do a cycle of folds and let rest another hour. Roll out with a rolling pin to a thickness of a couple centimeters (just under 1 inch). Cut out 6 square shapes measuring 6 x 6 cm (2.4 x 2.4 in). Place a generous spoonful of the filling in the middle of each square.
Close up the four sides of each square towards the middle, then turn over and arrange on a baking sheet lined with baking paper. Continue until all 6 *buchteln* are made, keeping them close to each other on the baking sheet.
Let rest for another couple of hours. Brush the surfaces with melted butter and bake in an oven heated to 180°C/355°F.
Bake for about 30 minutes. Remove from the oven and let cool, then dust with plenty of powdered sugar.

ALMOND AND CARROT *BOTTONCINI*

Carrot cake was one of my favorite regular snacks as a child. I loved that combination of flavor and sweetness, the flakiness of the almond flour, and its lively, playful color. These bottoncini, or little buttons, are a grown-up's version, being a healthy recipe very low in fats.

FOR **7-8** PIECES

75 g (2.7 oz) of fed starter
250 g (2 cups) all-purpose flour
150 ml (⅔ cup) carrot juice
150 g (1 & ½ cups) almond flour
75 g (⅓ cup) soy yogurt
50 g (2 & ⅓ tbsp) honey
25 ml (2 tbsp) extra virgin olive oil
A pinch of salt

TO DECORATE

100 g (¾ cup) powdered sugar
2 tsp carrot juice
7-8 shelled almonds

Combine the starter, carrot juice and honey until a smooth batter forms. While continuously working the mixture, add the flours followed by the yogurt, oil, and salt.
Work the dough thoroughly to obtain a dough as elastic and uniform as possible.
Let rise in a covered bowl for at least 6 hours, until doubled in volume.
Once the dough has leavened, form 7-8 balls weighing around 100 g (3.5 oz) each.
Arrange them in muffin tins and let rest for another 2 hours, covered.
Once risen sufficiently, bake at 180°C/355°F for about 25-30 minutes. Let cool.
Make a glaze by mixing the carrot juice and powdered sugar. Brush the glaze on the muffins and decorate with the almonds.

PANBRIOCHE WITH COCONUT MILK

The few ingredients in this recipe make for an exquisitely soft and fragrant bread, dairy- and egg-free, soon to become a regular feature at your breakfast table and come snack time.

FOR **1** *PANBRIOCHE* LOAF

60 g (2.1 oz) of fed starter
200 g (1 & ⅔ cups) all-purpose flour
200 ml (⅓ pt) coconut milk
30 g (¼ cup) brown sugar
A pinch of salt

Dissolve the starter in a bowl with the coconut milk.
Add the flour and begin to work the mixture. After a few minutes, add the sugar and salt and continue kneading for around ten minutes. Do not worry if the dough is liquid or sticky.
Let rise in a covered bowl for 4-5 hours.
Turn the dough out onto a well-floured work surface, using a spatula if needed. Do a cycle of book folds and shape into a loaf. Transfer to a plum cake loaf tin lined with baking paper and let rest another 2 hours, covered.
Preheat the oven to 180°C/355°F. Cover the tin with a sheet of aluminum foil, leaving a little space for expansion during baking. Bake for 20 minutes, remove the foil and continue baking for another 20 minutes at the same temperature.

SEMI-WHOLE WHEAT LOAF WITH MUESLI

*Do you love muesli for breakfast? If so, you will certainly enjoy this bread,
which brings together the sweetness of raisins and the richness of figs.
Serve with yogurt for a truly energized morning meal.*

FOR **3** PIECES

150 g (5.3 oz) of fed starter

500 g (4 & ⅛ cups) whole grain, stone-
    ground flour

200 g (1 & ⅔ cups) all-purpose flour

500 ml (2 cups) water

300 g (10.5 oz) muesli

100 g (⅔ cup) raisins

2 tsp salt

TO DECORATE

1 tbsp muesli

Soak the raisins in lukewarm water.

Meanwhile, dissolve the starter in the water. Slowly add the whole wheat flour, kneading until a very consistent dough forms.

Squeeze the water from the raisins, add to the dough along with the other ingredients (all-purpose flour, muesli, salt) and continue kneading.

Once the dough is formed, cover with a tea towel and let rise at room temperature for about 4-5 hours, until doubled in volume.

Work the dough on a floured work surface. Do a cycle of folds and let rest about another hour. Divide the dough and shape into three loaves, each approximately 600 g (21 oz) in weight.

Arrange the loaves on a baking sheet lined with baking paper and let rise for a couple of hours.

Before baking, score the loaves with a very sharp knife, brush them with a small amount of water and sprinkle with the muesli. Bake in an oven heated to 250°C/480°F for 15 minutes, then lower the heat to 200°C/390°F and bake for another 30 minutes.

BELGIAN *CRAMIQUE* WITH FIGS AND RUM

Belgium captured my heart the very first time I visited on holiday. And not only for the beer and French fries, but also for the wonderful sweets like this buttery, soft brioche, which here I have recreated with a few alterations from the original. The result is a delicious fig and rum bread that the bold of palate will love accompanied by savory cheeses.

FOR 1 *CRAMIQUE*

100 g (3.5 oz) of fed starter
350 g (2 & ¾ cups) all-purpose flour
130 ml (just over ½ cup) milk
100 g (3.5 oz) dried figs
70 g (5 tbsp) butter, softened
60 g (⅓ cup) brown sugar
1 egg
1 glass of rum
A pinch of salt

TO DECORATE
1 egg yolk
2 tbsp milk

Soak the dried figs in the rum for a couple hours. Remove and cut into cubes. Combine the starter and the milk. Add the flour, working with your hands. Halfway through the kneading, add the remaining ingredients (the figs and lastly the salt), and continue working the dough until compact and consistent yet elastic. Transfer to a bowl, cover with cling wrap, and let rise in the refrigerator for about 12 hours.

Remove from the fridge and let return to room temperature.

Do a cycle of folds and divide the dough into three equal parts. Shape each into a loaf about 30 cm (12 in) long. Braid the three pieces. Arrange the braid in a plum cake tin lined with baking paper.

Cover and let rise at room temperature for 3-4 hours. Beat the egg yolk and milk and brush over the surface.

Bake in an oven heated to 200°C/390°F for 10 minutes. Lower the temperature to 180°C/350°F and continue baking for another 20-30 minutes.

SOFT APPLE CAKE "BITES"

Here's a wee snack for wee hands. Like small bites of a delicious, homemade apple cake, these will have everyone in the house feeling like a kid again.

FOR **20** PIECES

100 g (3.5 oz) of fed starter
300 g (2 & ⅓ cups) all-purpose flour
150 ml (⅔ cup) water
100 g (⅔ cup) brown sugar
50 g (3 & ½ tbsp) butter
2 eggs
A pinch of salt

FOR THE FILLING

1 apple
1 tsp powdered cinnamon

Mix the starter and the water in a bowl. Add the flour and work with your hands until a uniform mixture forms.

Meanwhile, soften the butter at room temperature. Beat the eggs in a bowl.

Combine all the remaining ingredients in the bowl, including the salt, and begin to mix the dough. This might be a bit challenging at the beginning, given that you are adding semi-liquid ingredients to an already formed mixture. Yet it's important to continue kneading carefully until a homogeneous dough forms.

Let rise in a covered bowl for 5-6 hours.

In the meantime, peel the apple and cut into cubes. Place the apple in a bowl and add a generous spoonful of cinnamon.

Turn the dough out onto a floured work surface and work with your hands to form a loaf. Roll out the loaf with a rolling pin to a thickness of about .5 cm (.2 in).

Using a round ravioli press or cookie cutter, press out disks approximately 4-5 cm (1.5-2 in) in diameter. Arrange the disks on a baking sheet lined with baking paper. Place some of the apple filling on each disk. Moisten the edges of each and cover with a second disk to form a small stuffed pocket. Continue until all the disks are filled and sealed.

Cover and let rise another 2-3 hours.

Bake in an oven heated to 200°C/390°F for about 20 minutes.

When cool, dust with powdered sugar (optional).

BLUEBERRY PIE

This recipe came about one Sunday afternoon, with a steaming cup of tea in hand.
Its slightly sweet dough embodies all the flavors and memories of summer that blueberries bring.
I highly recommend that you choose a quality jam, one that tastes of fruit
rather than sugar—as this ingredient is the real star of this recipe.

FOR 1 PIE

80 g (2.9 oz) of fed starter
320 g (2 & ½ cups) all-purpose flour
160 ml (just over ⅔ cup) water
2 tbsp brown sugar
A pinch of salt

FOR THE FILLING

200 g (7 oz) blueberry jam

TO DECORATE

1 tbsp extra virgin olive oil
2 tbsp brown sugar

Dissolve the starter with the water in a bowl. Add the flour, sugar, and salt and knead thoroughly until a smooth, uniform mixture forms.

Cover and let rise for 5-6 hours, until doubled in volume.

Do a cycle of folds. Divide the dough into 2 equal parts, each weighing about 300 g (10.5 oz).

Lightly oil a pie dish 24 cm (9-10 in) in diameter and with high edges. Carefully press out the first piece of dough in the dish using your hands, as if you were making a focaccia bread.

Use a spoon to spread the blueberry jam over the surface.

Still using your hands, press out the second piece of dough on the work surface, forming a disk the same size as the first. Very carefully place the dough on top of the pie dish, being sure to cover all the jam. Seal the edges well.

Cover and let rise for a couple hours. Brush the surface with olive oil and dust with the brown sugar.

Bake in an oven preheated to 180°C/355°F for about 30 minutes.

BELGIAN CAKE

*Melted butter and caramelized sugar work their magic in this cake
with Flemish roots, forming a sweet, crunchy, fragrant top crust.
Go ahead and serve with a few squares of Belgian chocolate. I won't tell.*

FOR 1 CAKE

200 g (7 oz) of fed starter
300 g (2 & ⅓ cups) all-purpose flour
150 ml (⅔ cup) water
30 g (2 tbsp) butter, softened
30 g (¼ cup) brown sugar
A pinch of salt

TO DECORATE
2 tsp butter
2 tbsp brown sugar

Dissolve the starter in the water. Add the flour, followed by all the other ingredients while kneading to obtain a smooth, uniform dough.
Cover and let rise at room temperature for about 4 hours.
Transfer the dough to a work surface and do a cycle of folds. Let rest another hour, covered, then press the dough out on a baking sheet covered with baking paper. Let rest another 2 hours.
Decorate the surface with small flakes of butter. Dust with the sugar and bake in an oven preheated to 200°C/390°F for about 20 minutes.

SPICED BREAD WITH APPLES *EN PAPILLOTE*

I've always been fascinated by candied apples, all flaming red and sugary, catching my eye as I perused the stands at local street fairs. Yet in truth I never tasted one, being artificial and not very healthy. These apples, however, are special. Cooked en papillote—*enveloped in a warm, spiced dough—they are sure to have you dreaming of Christmas!*

FOR **3** PIECES

30 g (1 oz) of fed starter
100 g (¾ cup) all-purpose flour
50 ml (¼ cup) water
30 g (1 & ½ tbsp) honey
30 g (¼ cup) brown sugar
1 tsp ginger bread spices (nutmeg, cinnamon, clove)
1 tsp salt
3 small apples
1 tbsp raisins
1 tbsp pine nuts

Dissolve the starter in the water and begin to add the flour.
Knead quickly, then add the honey, sugar, spices and salt and continue working the dough until it has a very smooth and elastic consistency.
Cover and let rise at room temperature for 5-6 hours.
Turn the dough out onto a floured work surface. Using a rolling pin, roll out the dough to a thickness of .5 cm (.2 in).
In the meantime, wash and core the apples.
Place one apple at a time on the pastry. Fill the core of the apple with raisins and pine nuts. Cut a circle in the dough around the apple, big enough to close up the entire apple.
Close by bringing the pastry upwards and completely enveloping the fruit.
Arrange the wrapped apples on a baking sheet lined with baking paper and let rise for another couple of hours.
Bake in an oven preheated to 180°C/355°F for 40 minutes.

MINI VEGAN CROISSANTS WITH HAZELNUT CREAM

Making these soft, delicious croissants (or cornetti in Italian) brings great satisfaction, as the recipe is healthy, easy and quick. The hazelnut cream renders them tasty, flaky, and soft. Another treat you are likely to fight over at home!

FOR ABOUT 15 PIECES

50 g (1 oz) of fed starter
200 g (1 & ⅔ cups) all-purpose flour
100 ml (⅓ cup) water
60 g (2 oz/about 4 tbsp) pure hazelnut
  cream
2 tbsp brown sugar
A pinch of salt

FOR THE FILLING
2-3 tbsp brown sugar
1 tbsp unsweetened cocoa powder

Dissolve the starter in the water. Add the flour and begin to knead. Add the hazelnut cream along with the sugar and salt and continue working until a smooth, uniform dough forms. Cover and let rise for 4-5 hours, until doubled in volume. Transfer the dough to a floured work surface. Do a cycle of folds and let rest another hour. Using a rolling pin, roll the dough out as thinly as possible.
Use a knife to cut triangle shapes in the dough. Dust with a small amount of sugar and cocoa powder and roll the shapes up to form small croissants.
Cover and let rise for another two hours. Bake at 180°C/355°F for about 20 minutes.

RYE *PANBRULÉ* WITH DRIED FRUIT

Dried fruit, dehydrated apples and cinnamon lend a festive aroma to this sweet bread, one reminiscent of evenings relaxing after dinner in front of the fireplace. Rye flour with its typically Northern European touch renders this bread even more Christmas-y, yet in truth panbrulé is a bread for all seasons.

FOR 1 *PANBRULÉ*

100 g (3.5 oz) of fed starter
350 g (2 & ¾ cups) rye flour
170 ml (just under ¾ cup) water
30 g (¼ cup) raisins
30 g (1 oz circa) chopped walnuts
30 g (1 oz circa) dehydrated apples
1 tsp powdered cinnamon
1 tsp salt

Mix the starter in a bowl with the water. Add the rye flour and begin to knead using your hands.

Halfway through kneading, add the remaining ingredients. Keep working with both hands until a well-blended, slightly sticky dough forms.

Cover with a tea towel and let rise at room temperature for 4-5 hours, until doubled in volume.

Transfer the dough to a work surface. Do a cycle of book folds and shape into a low loaf. Place in a bread tin.

Cover the tin with a sheet of aluminum foil and let rest for a couple hours.

Bake in an oven preheated to 180°C/355°F for about one hour.

PAIN D'ÉPICES WITH CANDIED GINGER

In Belgium I visited some producers of pain d'épices, an experience that for some is akin to entering the "Chocolate Factory". The intensely spiced aromas of cinnamon, clove, ginger, and nutmeg filled the air, while jars of sweet, viscous honey were everywhere. It was poetry. Pure poetry. Let this pan take you on journey along the canals of Flanders. Is the tea ready?

FOR 1 *PAN D'ÉPICES* LOAF

70 g (2.5 oz) of fed starter
230 g (1 & ¾ cups) all-purpose flour
120 ml (just under ½ cup) water
70 g (3 & ⅓ tbsp) honey
70 g (½ cup) brown sugar
70 g (2.5 oz) candied ginger, cubed
2 tsp powdered ginger bread spices
    (nutmeg, cinnamon, clove)
1 tsp salt

Dissolve the starter in the water and begin to add the flour, kneading quickly. Shortly after, add the honey, sugar, ginger, spices, and salt. Continue working until you have a smooth, uniform dough.

Cover and let rise at room temperature for 5-6 hours.

Work the dough on a floured work surface with a cycle of folds and shape into a loaf. Transfer to a plum cake loaf tin lined with baking paper.

Let rise again until doubled in volume. Bake in an oven preheated to 180°C/355°F for about one hour.

VEGAN WHOLE WHEAT PANCAKES

Perfect for a relaxed Sunday breakfast, these pancakes were born from several ideas spinning in my head along with the desire to use some non-standard ingredients. We've all tried the "classic" version with maple syrup, of course. These somewhat "alternative" pancakes are sure to please just as much, and will be gone in an instant!

FOR **8** PIECES

50 g (1.75 oz) of fed starter
100 g (just under 1 cup) soft wheat or
   cake flour
170 ml (just under ¾ cup) water
1 tbsp honey
1 tbsp brown sugar
1 tsp cinnamon
1 tsp salt

FOR BAKING
Sunflower or coconut oil

Dissolve the starter in the water. Add the flour and all the other ingredients, mixing well with a spoon until a smooth batter forms.

Cover the bowl with cling wrap and carefully poke holes in the plastic with a toothpick, to allow the mixture to breath. Let rest at room temperature for 8-10 hours. Heat a small amount of oil in a non-stick pan. Pour half a ladle of the leavened batter (about 3 tablespoons) into the pan and cook 3 minutes circa on each side, until the pancake starts to bubble at the edges and take on a golden color on both sides.

Continue in this manner until you have used up the batter, oiling the pan in between each pancake. Serve warm, with maple syrup or a red fruit jam.

HERITAGE GRAIN LOAF WITH ALMONDS, HAZELNUTS, AND CHESTNUT HONEY

If you can, try to find farmers in your area who are working to protect biodiversity by cultivating ancient heritage grains and producing flours. Then head back to your kitchen to rediscover all the flavor of bread how it once was, here enriched with a tasty blend of almonds, hazelnuts, and honey. Take your time, and savor them slowly.

FOR 1 LOAF

130 g (4.6 oz) of fed starter

430 g (3 & ¾ cups) soft wheat, heritage grain flour (such as Gentilrosso, Frassineto, or similar)

220 ml (just under 1 cup) water

40 g (1.4 oz) shelled hazelnuts

40 g (1.4 oz) shelled almonds

20 g (1 tbsp) chestnut honey

1 tsp salt

Dissolve the starter in a bowl with the water.

Add the honey and flour and begin to knead. Continue working the dough, adding the hazelnuts, almonds, and lastly the salt. Thoroughly knead until you have a uniform, elastic dough.

Cover and let rise at room temperature for 5-6 hours. Then turn out the dough onto a floured work surface. Work with a cycle of clock folds and shape into a loaf. Let rest another 2 hours circa. Score the surface with a sharp knife, making a checkerboard design. Bake in an oven preheated to 250°C/480°F for the first 10 minutes, then lower the heat to 200°C/390°F and bake for another 40 minutes.

COCOA POWDER AND PEAR LOAF

FOR 1 LOAF

200 g (7 oz) of fed starter
500 g (4 cups) all-purpose flour
250 ml (1 cup) water
300 g (10.5 oz) pears, cut into small pieces
50 g (½ cup) cocoa powder
100 g (⅔ cup) brown sugar
1 tsp salt

Dissolve the starter in the water. Add the sugar and flour and begin to mix. Continue working the dough as you add the cocoa, the pears, and the salt, to obtain a dough that is smooth and uniform in consistency. Let rise in a covered bowl for 5-6 hours, until doubled in volume.

Turn the dough out onto a flour work surface and shape into a round loaf, using clock folds to help. Place the loaf on a sheet of baking paper and cover with a floured tea towel. Let rest another 2-3 hours.

Preheat the oven to max (250°C/480°F). Score the loaf with a cross shape. Bake for 15 minutes, then lower the temperature to 200°C/480°F and continue baking for about another 45 minutes.

PETITS GLAZED ROLLS WITH ALMONDS

*The crunchiness of almonds make these small rolls very tasty, perfect for any
kind of filling, from jams to chocolate. Let your taste buds run free!*

FOR 7-8 PIECES

120 g (4.2 oz) of fed starter
400 g (3 & ¼ cups) all-purpose flour
200 ml (⅓ pt) water
50 g (1.75 oz) almonds, roughly
    chopped
50 g (1.75 oz) agave syrup
1 tsp salt

TO DECORATE
2-3 tbsp powdered sugar
Water

Mix the starter in the water until dissolved almost completely. Add the agave syrup
and flour and begin to knead. About halfway through kneading, add the salt and
the almonds. Continue working the dough until elastic.
Cover and let rise at room temperature for 5-6 hours.
Halfway through the leavening time do a cycle of folds, then leave to continue
rising.
Divide the dough into 7-8 parts weighing approximately 100 g (3.5 oz) each. Shape
into small rolls and place on a baking sheet lined with baking paper. Cover with a
floured tea towel.
After about two hours, brush the surfaces with a small amount of water and
generously sprinkle with powdered sugar.
Bake in an oven preheated to 180°C/355°F for about 20 minutes.

LEMON-GLAZED RICE PUDDING BITES

Rice pudding, or rice cooked in milk with sugar and vanilla, is one of my favorite desserts. Here I have transformed this favorite into bite-sized rolls—a true comfort food! The sweetness of rice flour and milk, fragrant lemon and a final touch of glaze make these impossible to resist.

FOR **8** PIECES

75 g (2.65 oz) of fed starter
125 g (1 cup) all-purpose flour
150 g (1 cup) whole grain rice flour
125 ml (½ cup) milk
50 g (1.75 oz) agave syrup
1 tsp salt
Zest of 1 organic lemon

TO DECORATE

100 g (¾ cup) powdered sugar
Juice of ½ an organic lemon

Let the milk come to room temperature. Mix the starter in the milk until completely dissolved.

Add the two flours and while mixing add the syrup, salt, and lemon zest. Shape into a ball, cover and let rise for 4-5 hours, until doubled in volume.

Turn the dough out onto a floured work surface and do a cycle of folds. Let rest for another hour. Divide into 8 parts weighing approximately 60-70 g (2-2.5 oz) each and shape into small loaves. Transfer to a baking sheet lined with baking paper, cover with a lightly floured tea towel, and let rise for at least 2-3 hours.

Bake in an oven preheated to 200°C/390°F for about 20-25 minutes.

Let cool on a rack. Make the glaze by dissolving the powdered sugar in the lemon juice, and brush onto the pieces.

PASTIS BITES

Though I don't usually go in for hard alcohol, I do love the bottle designs. Which is why some years back I picked up a bottle of Pastis Ricard, with its gorgeous bottle as yellow as the Provencal sun, to use as a water carafe for our Sunday lunches. If you happen to love Pastis, however, these perfectly semi-sweet "bites" will evoke images of an aperitif taken with the old locals down at the port of Marseille.

FOR **12** PIECES

100 g (3.5 oz) of fed starter
250 g (2 cups) all-purpose flour
150 ml (⅔ cup) water
30 g (1 oz) soaked raisins
1 tbsp star anise seeds
A pinch of salt

Dissolve the starter in the water and slowly add the flour, mixing with your hands. Continue kneading and add the raisins and star anise and keep working the dough until it is smooth and uniform.
Cover and let rise for about 4-5 hours, until doubled in volume.
Do a cycle of folds and let the dough rest again. Shape the dough into small balls weighing approximately 50 g (1.75 oz) each.
Transfer the balls to small muffin tins and let rise another 2 hours circa.
Bake in an oven preheated to 180°C/355°F for about 20 minutes.

If I close my eyes, the aroma takes me back to childhood, a boy standing before the misty windows of a South Tyrolean pastry shop—where this cake is a steady feature. It's as pretty as it is tasty, and I promise you one slice will not be enough.

POPPY SEED STRUDEL

FOR 1 STRUDEL

150 g (5.3 oz) of fed starter
500 g (4 cups) all-purpose flour
125 ml (½ cup) milk
90 g (⅓ cup) butter
50 g (⅓ cup) brown sugar
1 whole egg + 2 yolks
A pinch of salt

FOR THE FILLING

240 g (8.5 oz) poppy seeds, chopped
200 ml (⅓ pt) milk
80 g (½ cup) brown sugar
20 g (1 & ⅓ tbsp) butter
1 tbsp acacia flower honey
1 tsp powdered cinnamon

TO DECORATE

1 egg yolk
2 tbsp milk

Pour the flour onto a work surface and make a "basin" by forming a hole in the middle. Add the starter to the middle of the hole along with the milk and dissolve. Add the egg and the egg yolks and use a fork to make a soft dough.
Add the butter, softened and in pieces, along with the sugar and salt.
Knead all the ingredients together with the flour and form a ball shape. Transfer to a bowl, cover and let rise at room temperature for about 6 hours. The dough will double in volume.
In the meanwhile, bring the ingredients for the filling, excluding the honey, to boil in a small pot. Remove from the heat, let cool, and add the honey. Mix well.
Now punch down the risen dough and do a cycle of folds on a floured work surface. Press out the dough with your hands into a rectangle sheet about 2 cm thick (.8 in).
Pour the filling on top, leaving a border of about 2 cm (.8 in). Moisten the edge slightly with a small amount of milk.
Roll up the strudel from the longest side and fold in the edges towards the bottom. Place on a baking sheet lined with baking paper. Cover and let rise for another 2 hours circa.
Beat the egg yolks with 2 tablespoons of milk. Brush on the strudel and bake at 180°C/355°F for around 35-40 minutes.

WHITE PEACH AND HAZELNUT *TARTE TATIN*

The intoxicating aroma of these tatin recalls just-gathered summer fruits, while the warm, velvety filling releases a deliciously sweet juice. This is a simple dessert, yet one hard to forget.

FOR **8** PIECES

50 g (1.75 oz) of fed starter
200 g (1 & ⅔ cups) all-purpose flour
100 ml (⅓ cup) water
50 g (about 2 oz/4 tbsp) pure hazelnut
  cream
1 tbsp brown sugar
A pinch of salt

FOR THE FILLING

5 white peaches
3 tbsp brown sugar
30 g (2 tbsp) butter

Dissolve the fed starter in the water. Add the flour and begin to work the mixture. Add the hazelnut cream along with the sugar, and salt and continue working until a smooth, uniform dough forms. Let rise in a covered bowl for about 4 hours.

In the meantime, slice the peaches. Heat the butter and sugar in a pan until slightly golden. Add the peaches and caramelize on both sides.

Grease the *tatin* tins with butter. Add the peaches to the bottom of tins and let cool.

When the dough has risen, roll it out onto a floured work surface. Do a cycle of folds and let rest. Using a rolling pin, next roll the dough to a thickness of about 1-2 cm (.4-.8 in).

Cut discs out of the dough measuring the same diameter as the tins. Cover the peaches with the dough discs, making sure the dough adheres to the peaches and the edges are well sealed.

Let rest for another hour circa. Bake for 20 minutes at 180°C/355°F. Cool completely and then turn them out carefully.

SWEET SPELT FLOUR BRAID WITH RAISINS

After several attempts, here is my recipe for a perfect brioche dough, which with just a few cuts blooms in a manner marvelous to behold. The spelt flour lends this braided loaf something extra special, too.

FOR 1 BRAIDED LOAF

150 g (5.3 oz) of fed starter
500 g (5 cups) white spelt flour
125 ml (½ cup) milk
100 g (½ cup) butter
60 g (⅓ cup) brown sugar
1 whole egg + 2 yolks
1 tsp salt

FOR THE FILLING

100 g (3.5 oz) soaked raisins
50 g (¼ cup) butter
2 tbsp brown sugar

TO DECORATE

1 egg yolk
2 tbsp milk

Pour the flour onto a work surface and make a "basin" by forming a hole in the middle. Add the starter in the middle of the hole along with the lukewarm milk and dissolve. Add the egg and the egg yolks and use a fork to make a soft dough. Add the butter, softened and in pieces, along with the sugar and salt.

Knead all the ingredients together with the flour to form a ball shape. Transfer to a bowl, cover and let rise at room temperature for about 6 hours. The dough will double in volume.

Next press out the leavened dough with your hands. Do a cycle of book folds and let rest. Using a rolling pin, roll out the dough to a rectangle shape to a thickness of about 1 cm (.4 in). Melt the butter and brush on top of the dough. Sprinkle on the raisins and the sugar.

Roll up the dough from the longest side, forming a tight, long roll.

With a thin-edged, very sharp knife cut the roll in half lengthwise. Separate the two pieces. Keeping the cut sides facing upwards, begin to braid the two pieces.

Press the ends together well to seal them and place the braid on a baking sheet lined with baking paper. Let rise for another 2 hours in a slightly warm place. Beat the egg yolks with the milk and brush on top of the roll. Bake in an oven preheated to 180°C/355°F for about 30-40 minutes.

BITE-SIZED MORSELS

In the blink of an eye, these crispy, perfectly flavored crackers, breadsticks, mini rolls and other delicious morsels will lure you into an irresistible tunnel of snacking. Before you know it, you'll be proclaiming, "Just one more!". Famous last words, right?

BAGELS

Is there anything like a toasted bagel? Preferably one sliced in half and filled with mustard, lettuce, aged cheese and smoked prosciutto cotto. Take this with you to work for your lunch, ideally spent comfortably seated on a bench in the midday sun, and all will be right in your world.

FOR **10** PIECES

150 g (5.3 oz) of fed starter
500 g (4 cups) all-purpose flour
250 ml (1 cup) water
50 ml (3 & ½ tbsp) extra virgin olive oil
25 g (3 tbsp) unrefined cane sugar
2 tsp salt

TO DECORATE

1 egg
5 tsp mixed seeds (sesame, pumpkin,
   flax, sunflower, poppy)

Dissolve the starter in the water and begin to add the flour, kneading with your hands. Shortly after, mix in the oil, sugar, and salt and continue working the dough until well combined and smooth.

Let rise at room temperature in a covered bowl for about 5 hours, until doubled in volume.

Do a cycle of folds and form ten ball shapes weighing 100 g (3.5 oz) each. Let rest another hour.

In the meantime, bring a large amount of water to the boil in a low, wide pot.

Using your finger, make a hole inside each of the dough balls, then boil for about one minute. Remove quickly from the water and place on a baking sheet lined with baking paper.

Beat the egg, diluting with a bit of water if needed. Brush this onto the bagels and sprinkle generously with the mixed seeds.

Bake in an oven preheated to 180°C/355°F for 20-30 minutes.

Tired of the usual bread basket? These baked breadsticks are the answer. Delicious just out of the oven, fragrant and warm, they're great for munching before, during, and even after mealtime.

CORN FLOUR BREAD STICKS

FOR **15** PIECES

60 g (2.1 oz) of fed starter
140 g (1 & ⅛ cups) all-purpose flour
60 g (½ cup) coarse grain corn flour
100 ml (⅓ cup) water
40 ml (3 tbsp) extra virgin olive oil
1 tsp salt

TO DECORATE
4 tsp coarse grain corn flour

Dissolve the starter in the water. Add the two flours and begin to knead. Halfway through kneading, add the salt and the oil, and continue working the dough until a well-combined, elastic dough forms.
Let rise in a covered bowl for 4-5 hours, until doubled in volume.
Turn the dough out onto a floured work surface. Divide into 15 equal parts.
Dust the work surface with a generous amount of the corn flour. Roll out each piece of dough, pressing with the tips of your fingers to form bread sticks about 20 cm (8 in) long.
Carefully arrange the bread sticks on a baking sheet lined with baking paper and let rest for about another 2 hours.
Bake in an oven preheated to 200°C/390°F for about 25 minutes.

CHICKPEA FLOUR *CIAPPE*

This unexpected snack is a twist on the classic Italian ciappa *(a flatbread similar to a* piadina *or* tortilla*), with an added touch of chickpea flour. It's love at first bite. Try them with a soft cheese like crescenza and you'll be transported to Liguria.*

FOR ABOUT **15** PIECES

60 g (2.1 oz) of fed starter
100 g (¾ cup) all-purpose flour
100 g (1 & ⅛ cups) chickpea flour
130 ml (just over ½ cup) water
20 g (1 & ½ tbsp) extra virgin olive oil
1 tsp salt

Dissolve the starter in the water. Add the two flours and begin to knead. Then add the oil and the salt, working the dough into a smooth loaf.
Cover and let rest at room temperature for about 5 hours.
Once leavened, turn the dough out onto a floured work surface. Roll out with a rolling pin to as thin as possible.
Use a knife to cut out rectangle shapes about 15 cm (6 in) long and 5 cm (2 in) wide. Arrange on a baking sheet lined with baking paper.
Let rest for another hour. Poke holes in the *ciappe* with the tines of a fork and bake for 10 minutes at 250°C/480°F.

SPELT FLOUR CRACKERS

These rustic, comforting little crackers, reminiscent of country aromas and summertime snacks under the veranda, are best paired with mixed seasonal vegetables and a cold beer. A snack you never have to feel guilty about.

FOR ABOUT **30** PIECES

40 g (1.4 oz) of fed starter
130 g (1 & ½ cups) white spelt flour
70 ml (just over ¼ cup) water
10 ml (2 & ¼ tsp) extra virgin olive oil
1 tsp salt

TO DECORATE
2 tsp spelt (or farro) flakes

Dissolve the starter in the water. Add the flour and begin to combine.
Shortly after, add the oil and the salt, and keep working the dough until it is very smooth.
Let rise at room temperature for 3-4 hours.
Lightly flour a piece of baking paper. Using a rolling pin, roll the dough out on the paper to a thin sheet. Cut out small squares using a wavy-edged pastry wheel.
Puncture the surfaces using the tines of a fork. Brush on a small amount of water and dust generously with the flakes.
Leave on the baking paper and let rise for another couple of hours. Bake in an oven preheated to 180°C/355°F for 15 minutes.

GALLETTI WATER CRACKERS

Once on vacation in Malta, while searching out interesting local breads as usual, I came across these "galletti" crackers (galletto means cockerel in Italian). Likely related to our water crackers or biscuits, these simple crackers go perfectly with cheeses, dips, and vegetables, accompanied by a nice glass of chilled wine. The following recipe is my playful interpretation of the so-called "rooster crackers".

FOR ABOUT **50** PIECES

50 g (1.75 oz) of fed starter
500 g (2 cups) whole grain,
    stone-ground flour
125 ml (½ cup) water

Dissolve the starter in the water. Add the flour, kneading well until a smooth and uniform dough forms.
Cover with a tea towel and let rise at room temperature about 4-5 hours, until doubled in volume.
Roll the dough out on a floured work surface to a very thin sheet, using a rolling pin.
To make the crackers, try to find a cookie cutter in the shape of a rooster.
Otherwise use any other type of cookie cutter. Press out the crackers and place on a baking sheet lined with baking paper.
Use the tines of a fork to lightly puncture each cracker. Bake in an oven preheated to 190°C/375°F for about 15 minutes.

LAUGENBROT

It's impossible not to love pretzels. The traditional German method of using caustic soda in the first stage (in homes and in this recipe substituted with the safer solution of water and baking soda) is known as Laugengebäck, and it's what gives pretzels their color, crunch, and unparalleled flavor. Prepared according to the same method, these small breads called Laugenbrot are decorated with mixed seeds. To me they have always represented a tempting reason to move to Germany. Along with German beer, naturally.

FOR **10** PIECES

120 g (4 oz) of fed starter
400 g (3 & ¼ cups) all-purpose flour
200 ml (⅓ pt) water
50 ml (3 & ⅔ tbsp) extra virgin olive
  oil, or 60 g (¼ cup) softened butter
1 tsp salt

FOR BOILING

1 l (4 cups) water
8 tsp baking soda
A pinch of salt

TO DECORATE

1 tbsp coarse salt
1 tbsp sesame seeds
1 tbsp pumpkin seeds

Mix the starter with the water in a bowl until dissolved. Next add the flour and begin to knead, using your hands. Shortly after, mix in the oil (or butter) and the salt, working the dough for a few minutes more.

Let rise in a covered bowl for 5-6 hours, until doubled in size.

Transfer the dough to a work surface. Do a cycle of folds and let rest. Divide the dough into 10 equal parts weighing around 80 g (3 oz) each. Shape into balls and let rise on a floured work surface for another hour circa.

Meanwhile, heat the oven to 200°C/390°F. Fill a wide, low pot with the water, baking soda, and a pinch of salt.

Bring the water to the boil. Add the dough shapes one at a time to the water and boil for one minute. Drain using a skimmer and transfer to a baking sheet lined with baking paper.

Score the surfaces with a razor blade or very sharp knife and decorate with the seeds and/or coarse salt.

Bake in an oven preheated to 200°C/390°F for 25 minutes.

MINI SCHÜTTELBROT

I remember bringing these small rye crackers along on my mountain walks, and they still remind me Alpine mountains, pastures, and flowers. Tasty and perfect for munching on come break time, they go well with cured meats and malga cheeses, those traditionally made in Alpine cottages.

FOR AROUND **50** MINI *SCHÜTTELBROT*

150 g (5.3 oz) of fed starter
450 g (3 & ½ cups) rye flour
400 ml (1 & ⅔ cups) water
2 tsp salt
1 tsp mixed herbs for rye breads
   (caraway, fenugreek, fennel)

Dissolve the starter in the water. Add the flour and begin to combine using a wooden spoon.
The dough will be very hydrated. Keep kneading, adding the remaining ingredients and then let rise in a covered bowl for around 5-6 hours.
Flour your hands well and make small shapes with the dough. Arrange on a baking sheet lined with baking paper. If the dough is too sticky to work, add another spoonful of flour.
Let rest for another two hours. Bake in an oven preheated to 200°C/390°F for around 20 minutes.

SEMI-SWEET FLAXSEED ROLLS

*These rolls debuted at a friend's baptism celebration for her daughter,
where they were a huge hit filled with olive pesto and pecorino cheese.
Try them with other ingredients of your choice for a delicious snack.*

FOR **30** PIECES

250 g (8.8 oz) of fed starter
700 g (5 & ⅔ cups) all-purpose or
    Italian type '0' flour
250 ml (1 cup) water
150 ml (⅔ cup) milk
150 ml (⅔ cup) extra virgin olive oil
80 g (⅓ cup) unrefined cane sugar
15 g (¾ tbsp) salt
3 tbsp golden flax seeds

TO DECORATE
3 tbsp golden flax seeds

Dissolve the starter in the water and milk in a bowl.
Add the flax seeds, sugar, and the flour and begin to knead.
While kneading, add the salt and the oil and continue working the mixture for about ten minutes, until the dough is smooth, well-combined and slightly sticky.
Cover and let rise for at least 5 hours, until doubled in volume.
Work the dough with a cycle of folds and let rest again, covered. Divide the dough and form ball shapes, each weighing approximately 30 g (1 oz). Transfer to a baking sheet lined with baking paper.
Brush the surfaces with water and sprinkle on the seeds. Let rest another couple of hours and bake at 180°C/355°F for 15 minutes.

MINI PARMESAN ROLLS

Along the road behind my high school in Bologna was the historic bakery belonging to the Simili sisters—a true Bolognese institution for locals and visitors alike, anyone who loved bread and baked goods. One of their specialties were these "parmigianni", super tasty morsels made with a semi-sweet dough and parmesan cheese, which I loved to snack on while strolling under the porticoes of Bologna. They were so good in fact, I'd forget all about the rain.

FOR **30** PIECES

250 g (8.8 oz) of fed starter
700 g (5 & ⅔ cups) all-purpose or
  Italian type '0' flour
350 ml (1 & ⅓ cups) water
200 g (2 cups) grated parmesan cheese
150 g (⅔ cup) butter
80 g (⅓ cup) unrefined cane sugar
15 g (¾ tbsp) salt

TO DECORATE

1 egg

Dissolve the starter in a bowl with the water. Add the sugar and the flour and begin to knead.

While kneading, add the salt and the butter (softened) and continue working the mixture for about ten minutes, until the dough is smooth, well-combined and slightly sticky.

Cover and let rise for at least 5-6 hours, until doubled in volume.

Roll the dough out onto a work surface and do a cycle of folds. Form a rectangle shape and dust generously with the grated cheese, making sure to cover the entire surface. Roll the dough into a loaf shape and then slice into small rounds.

Arrange the rounds on a baking sheet lined with baking paper and let rest for another couple hours. Beat the egg and brush it on the surfaces of the rolls. Bake in an oven preheated to 180°C/355°F for 15 minutes.

OLIVE OIL *PIADINE*

For me, piadine are the food of the Gods. This classic Italian (and international) street food is wonderful warm, filled with ingredients or on their own. Somehow piadine make everything right in the world, even on a rainy day. This recipe with sourdough starter is not, strictly speaking, accurate. And while a true Romagna native would probably scoff, they must be tasted all the same. Taste for yourself.

FOR **3** PIECES

70 g (2.5 oz) of fed starter
230 g (1 & ¾ cups) all-purpose flour
120 ml (just under ½ cup) water
50 ml (3 & ⅔ tbsp) extra virgin olive oil
1 tsp salt

Dissolve the starter in the water. Add the flour and begin to knead.
Halfway through kneading, mix in the oil and the salt and work the dough thoroughly until it is very elastic and homogeneous.
Cover in a bowl and let rise at room temperature for 5-6 hours.
Divide the dough into three equal ball shapes weighing about 150 g (5 oz) each.
In the meantime, heat a nonstick pan on the stove top.
On a well-floured work surface, roll out each ball with a rolling pin to form a round the same size as your pan.
Cook the piadine one at a time for a few minutes on each side, until they are nicely cooked but not too dry.
Fill them with ingredients of your choice and enjoy while still warm.

SWEET PAPRIKA *PICOS*

Whenever you have a few extra beers in the fridge, these crunchy and flavorful picos are a great reason to invite some friends over. They're truly irresistible, bite after bite. Who's ready to watch the game?

FOR ABOUT 40 PIECES

70 g (2.5 oz) of fed starter
270 g (2 & ⅛ cups) all-purpose or
    Italian type '0' flour
130 ml (just over ½ cup) water
30 ml (2 & ¼ tbsp) extra virgin olive oil
A pinch of salt

TO DECORATE

1 tbsp coarse salt
1 tsp powdered sweet paprika

Dissolve the starter in the water. Add the flour and begin to knead.
Continue working the dough, and meanwhile add the oil and the salt, until very smooth.
Transfer to a bowl, cover and let rise at room temperature for about 4-5 hours. Turn the dough out onto a floured work surface and shape in small loaves about 1 cm in diameter (.4 in). Cut these into pieces 5-6 cm in length (2-2.5 in).
Close up the ends to form a knot shape. Arrange on a baking sheet lined with baking paper. Let rest for a couple of hours. Brush carefully with a small amount of water and sprinkle with a bit of coarse salt and plenty of sweet paprika.
Bake at 200°C/390°F for 20 minutes.

SAMOSAS WITH EGGPLANT AND GREEN LENTIL CREAM

These samosas are only like the Indian version in name, inspired by Indian ingredients and seasonings like those bundled inside these bread wraps. Serve at your next Indian feast.

FOR **10** SAMOSAS

80 g (2.8 oz) of fed starter
250 g (2 cups) all-purpose or Italian
    type '0' flour
130 ml (just over ½ cup) water
40 ml (3 tbsp) extra virgin olive oil
1 tsp salt

FOR THE FILLING
1 eggplant
1 spring onion
50 g (¼ cup) dried green lentils
1 tsp curry powder
Extra virgin olive oil

Cook the lentils in 150 ml (⅔ cup) water in a small pan, covered, for about 15 minutes, until all the liquid has been cooked off.

Chop the onion and sauté in a nonstick pan with a small amount of oil.

Rinse the eggplant and cut into cubes. Add the eggplant to the onion and cook until soft.

Use an immersion blender to process the eggplant mixture into a cream. Add the cooked lentils to the mixture along with the curry powder and combine well. Let cool.

Dissolve the starter in the water in a bowl. Add the flour and continue kneading as you add the salt and the oil. Work the dough thoroughly until homogeneous. Cover and let rise for about 5 hours.

Transfer the dough to a floured work surface and divide into 10 balls, each weighing approximately 50 g (1.75 oz).

Roll each ball out with a rolling pin to form squares with sides measuring 10 cm circa (4 in).

Divide each piece diagonally into two equal parts. Fill one part with a spoonful of the filling. Close the triangle with the other piece of dough and carefully seal the edges.

Place the samosas on a baking sheet lined with baking paper and let rest another hour.

Brush the tops with a small amount of extra virgin olive oil and bake at 200°C/390°F for about 20 minutes.

SWEDISH *SKORPOR* WITH CARDAMOM

These take me right back to Sweden, where it has just stopped snowing. The sun is shining, and the sky is blue. The roads are covered in white, while I sit inside a coffee shop listening to indie music and enjoying a breakfast of red berry jam with these cardamom Skorpor. Fragrant butter is the hidden star of this recipe, as it underscores the spiced aroma and flavor of the jam.

FOR **24** PIECES

80 g (2.8 oz) of fed starter
280 g (2 & ⅓ cups) whole wheat flour
140 ml (just under ⅔ cup) water
50 g (3 & ½ tbsp) butter, softened
30 g (3 tbsp) unrefined cane sugar
1 tsp salt
1 tsp crushed cardamom seeds

Dissolve the starter in the water. Add the flour and begin to knead. Shortly after, add the sugar, butter, cardamom seeds and lastly the salt. Work the dough thoroughly until smooth and homogeneous.

Transfer the dough to a bowl, cover and let rise for 5-6 hours.

Do a cycle of folds. Divide the dough into 12 equal parts, each weighing about 50 g (1.75 oz). Shape each piece into a small, elongated loaf and arrange them on a baking sheet lined with baking paper. Let rise for another 2 hours.

Meanwhile, heat the oven to 220°C/430°F and bake the loaves for 20 minutes. Remove from the oven and cut in half horizontally while still warm, using a very sharp knife.

Place all the sliced halves back on the baking sheet with the insides facing up.

Return to the oven and bake for another 30 minutes at 180°C/355°F. Remove from the oven and let cool completely.

POTATO *SUPPLÌ* WITH VENETO SOPPRESSA

Supplì are little "surprises" to enjoy while still warm, with their crunchy fried outer layer and soft, creamy, yummy potato filling. Here I have paired them with something unusual, bechamel and soppressa, a soft salami from the Veneto area, for a surprisingly delicious result.

FOR **10-12** PIECES

100 g (3.5 oz) of fed starter
300 g (2 & ⅓ cups) all-purpose or
    Italian type '0' flour
200 g (7 oz) potatoes
30 g (2 tbsp) butter
1 egg
1 tbsp milk
1 tsp salt

FOR THE FILLING
50 g (1.75 oz) soppressa salami from
    Veneto (or similar)
A dab of butter
1 tbsp flour
½ cup milk
1 tbsp grated Parmesan
1 tsp ground nutmeg

FOR FRYING
Extra virgin olive oil

Boil the potatoes, mash and let cool.

Dissolve the starter in the water. Add the flour and begin to knead. Continue kneading as you mix in the potato, softened butter, egg, milk, and salt, working the dough until soft.

Let rise in a covered bowl for about 5 hours.

In the meantime, make a thick bechamel. Melt the butter in a small pot. Add the flour and toast, stirring continuously. Add the milk, stirring briskly to prevent clumps. Bring to the boil just enough to thicken. Add the grated cheese and the nutmeg to the mixture.

Cut the salami into cubes.

Once leavened, punch down the dough and do a cycle of folds. Divide into small ball shapes weighing approximately 40-50 g (1.4-1.75 oz).

Press into each ball with your thumb to form a hole and fill with the bechamel and cubed salami.

Close the dough balls back up and seal well.

Heat the oil in a deep pan and fry a few pieces at a time until golden. Transfer to paper towels to allow excess oil to drain off. Serve warm.

WHOLE WHEAT BRAIDS WITH PISTACHIOS

As healthy as whole wheat and as tasty as the added pistachios, these braids are perfect for pairing with sweet or salty items, or simply to munch on by themselves.
A sinful treat, but in moderation.

FOR ABOUT **18-20** PIECES

50 g (1.75 oz) of fed starter
150 g (1 & ¼ cups) whole wheat flour
70 ml (just over ¼ cup) water
40 ml (3 tbsp) extra virgin olive oil
50 g (1.75 oz) shelled pistachios
1 tsp salt

Lightly grind the pistachios in a mortar.
Dissolve the starter in the water and begin to add the flour.
Knead with your hands, then mix in (in this order): the oil, pistachios, and salt.
Continue working to obtain an elastic, smooth, homogeneous dough.
Let rise in a covered bowl for 5-6 hours. Transfer to a floured work surface and form several small portions of about 20-30 g (.7-1 oz) each.
Flatten out each piece with your fingers to form a small rod shape. Fold in half and twist into a braid shape.
Heat the oven to 220°C/430°F. Transfer the braids to a baking sheet lined with baking paper. Bake for about 20 minutes.

GINGER AND RED CHILI PEPPER *TARALLINI*

Here's another irresistible bite-sized snack. Not much else is needed to explain these red chili taralli, the most Southern savory delicacy there is. A spoonful of ginger is added to render them even more spicy and tempting. For the brave of palate.

FOR ABOUT **40** PIECES

50 g (1.75 oz) of fed starter
200 g (2 & ⅔ cups) all-purpose or
    Italian type '0' flour
100 ml (⅓ cup) water
100 ml (½ cup) extra virgin olive oil
1 tsp ginger powder
1 tsp red chili powder
1 tsp salt

FOR BOILING
1 l (4 cups) water

Dissolve the starter in a bowl with the water. Add the flour and begin to work the mixture.

Shortly after, add the remaining ingredients and combine thoroughly.

Let rise in a covered bowl for 4-5 hours, until doubled in volume.

Turn the dough out onto a floured work surface. Use your hands to form *tarallini* shapes: take a small handful of dough, shape into a thin loaf about 3-4 cm (1-1.5 in) in length, and close up the ends in a ring shape.

In the meantime, bring a large amount of water to the boil in a low, wide pot.

Boil the *tarallini* for about one minute and remove from the water with a skimmer as soon as they rise to the surface.

Arrange the shapes on a baking sheet lined with baking paper. Bake for 30-40 minutes at 200°C/390°F.

SPELT AND *CIAUSCOLO* SALAMI *TORCETTI*

I returned home from a holiday in the Marche region with some of this unusually soft, decidedly flavorful salami known as ciauscolo. *Where else could it have ended up but in a bread recipe? Here is the result: thick bread sticks, crunchy on the outside and soft and fragrant within, known as* torcetti.

FOR ABOUT **20** PIECES

200 g (7 oz) of fed starter
500 g (5 cups) white spelt flour
250 ml (1 cup) water
200 g (7 oz) *ciauscolo* salami, or a similar fresh, very soft type of Italian salami
1 tsp salt

Dissolve the starter in the water. Add the flour and begin to knead. Crumble the salami. About halfway through kneading, add the salt and the salami to the dough and combine until a homogeneous dough forms.

Cover with a tea towel and let rise at room temperature for about 5-6 hours.

Transfer the dough to a floured work surface. Do a cycle of folds. Next form several rod shapes and press out with the palms of your hands to about 20 cm (8 in) in length.

Arrange on a baking sheet lined with baking paper. Roll into bread stick shapes and let rest for another couple hours.

Bake in an oven preheated to 200°C/390°F for about 20 minutes.

TOMATO AND DRIED RED PEPPER SPIRALS

The extremely addicting dried peppers used here known as cruschi *hail from the Basilicata region of Italy. They lend a unique quality to these spirals, which are sure to stimulate the appetite or possibly have you snacking without end.*

FOR **30** PIECES

100 g (3.5 oz) of fed starter
350 g (just over 2 cups) durum wheat
    semolina flour
170 ml (just under ¾ cup) water
1 tbsp extra virgin olive oil
1 tsp salt

FOR THE FILLING

2 tbsp tomato puree
1 tbsp extra virgin olive oil
30 g (1 oz) Cruschi peppers, chopped
Dried oregano

Dissolve the starter in the water and add the flour.
Knead thoroughly until a homogeneous dough forms. Add the salt and oil and continue working the dough.
Let rise in a covered bowl until doubled in volume (about 4-6 hours).
Using a rolling pin, roll the dough out on a floured work surface to a very thin rectangular sheet (about .5 cm or .2 in thickness).
Combine the tomato puree, oil, oregano, and dried peppers in a bowl.
Use a spoon to spread some of the mixture on half of the sheet of rolled out dough.
Fold the uncovered half over the half with tomato.
Cut strips of dough about 2 or 3 cm wide (about 1 in). Twist to form spiral shapes.
Arrange the spirals on a baking sheet lined with baking paper. Cover and let rise for one hour. Bake in an oven preheated to 180°C/355°F for 20-25 minutes.

WHOLE WHEAT PROVENCAL *ZEPPOLINE*

Try these for a late spring aperitif on the terrace. Reminiscent of grandpa's garden-fresh zucchini and pots of aromatic herbs, they're easy and quick to prepare, leaving you time to relax outside come sunset, with a lovely glass of wine.

FOR **20** PIECES

50 g (1.75 oz) of fed starter
100 g (¾ cup) whole wheat flour
80 ml (just under ⅓ cup) water
2 zucchini, grated
1 tbsp pitted black olives
1 tbsp mixed herbs de provence,
   chopped (thyme, sage, marjoram,
   oregano, etc.)
A pinch of salt

FOR FRYING
Delicate extra virgin olive oil

Prepare a leavened batter. In a bowl dissolve the starter in the water and add all the other ingredients. Let rise at room temperature in a covered bowl for about 4 hours. Heat the extra virgin olive oil in a pot. Drop a spoonful of the batter into the hot oil, using an additional spoon if needed. Fry a few pieces at a time, turning them so they turn golden on all sides (about 5 minutes).
Remove from the oil and dry on paper towels. Dust with salt and enjoy while still warm.

PIZZA AND FOCACCIA

There's nothing like the familiar aroma of a rich, delicious homemade dough, and pizza and focaccia are particularly satisfying, welcoming and comforting with every bite.

This simple recipe is an excellent way to use up that extra starter after a feeding, quick to prepare and truly tasty. Use either a fed starter or one that's been stored in the refrigerator for a few days.

ROSEMARY FOCACCIA

ROSEMARY FOCACCIA

FOR 1 FOCACCIA

300 g (10.5 oz) of fed starter

FOR THE TOPPING
4 tbsp extra virgin olive oil
1 tbsp coarse salt
1 tbsp chopped rosemary

Grease a round baking sheet with 2 tablespoons of oil. Press the starter dough out on sheet to a thickness of about 1 cm (.4 in).
Brush the surface with the remaining extra virgin olive oil and dust generously with the coarse salt and the rosemary.
Bake for 20 minutes at 200°C/390°F. Serve warm.

FOCACCIA WITH PINE NUT PESTO AND WILD GARLIC

FOR 1 FOCACCIA

50 g (1.75 oz) of fed starter
100 g (1 & ⅔ cups) semi-whole wheat flour
130 ml (just over ½ cup) water
A pinch of salt

FOR THE TOPPING
30 g (1 oz) pine nuts
30 g (1 oz) ricotta
30 g (1 oz) parmesan cheese
Extra virgin olive oil
1 tsp dried wild garlic

Dissolve the starter in the water. Add the flour and begin to knead.
Next add the salt and continue working the dough thoroughly.
Let rise at room temperature for 4-5 hours. Turn the dough out onto a floured work surface and do a series of clock folds.
Generously grease a baking sheet 28 cm (11 in) in diameter with extra virgin olive oil (or line with baking paper). Using your hands, press the dough out onto the baking sheet.
Let rest for about another 2 hours.
In the meantime, prepare the topping. Grind the pine nuts in a mortar, adding the ricotta and the parmesan. Lastly, drizzle in the olive oil.
Heat the oven to 250°C/480°F. Just before placing in the oven, delicately brush the focaccia surface with more extra virgin olive oil.
Bake for 15 minutes. Remove from the oven and quickly spread on the pesto and dust on the dried wild garlic. Return to the oven and continue baking for another 3 minutes.
Top with a handful of pine nuts (optional).

WHOLE WHEAT LIGURIAN *FUGASSA*

FOR 1 *FUGASSA* (FOCACCIA IN THE GENOESE DIALECT)

50 g (1.75 oz) of fed starter
250 g (2 & ⅛ cups) whole wheat flour
150 ml (⅔ cup) water
1 tbsp extra virgin olive oil
1 tsp sea salt

FOR THE TOPPING
4 tbsp extra virgin olive oil
1 tbsp coarse salt

Dissolve the starter in the water and add the oil, flour, and salt, kneading thoroughly until a homogeneous and well-hydrated dough forms.
Cover and let rest for 5-6 hours, until doubled in volume.
Grease a baking sheet. Turn the dough out onto the sheet and press well with your hands.
Cover the *fugassa* and let rise for another couple hours. Then brush the surface with oil and sprinkle on the salt.
Bake in an oven preheated to 250°C/480°F for about 20 minutes.

The pairing of wild garlic and pesto produces an intriguing flavor for this focaccia, one that will transport you to the seaside, breathing in the sea air, with your feet in the sand.

FOCACCIA WITH PINE NUT PESTO
AND WILD GARLIC

As is likely obvious by now, I enjoy re-working traditional recipes like baguettes and pizza using whole grain flours, especially organic, stone-ground flours. More than a mere trend, this choice is about flavor—the flavors of the earth and the countryside in particular. It's also a way to preserve the traditions of our grandparents and appreciate abundance through the authentic taste of freshly harvested ground wheat. As an added plus, it's good for you!

WHOLE WHEAT LIGURIAN *FUGASSA*

FOCACCIA WITH TRADITIONAL GENOESE PESTO

Once when my son was asked what he wants to be when he grows up, he responded, "pesto!"
He was not yet two years old, yet the marvelous flavor and aroma of Genoese pesto had already left its mark on his young taste buds. This recipe's combination of ingredients evokes the aroma of garden-fresh basil and a grove of lemon trees. Who knows? Perhaps in a few years it will include my son's own pesto. This recipe calls for potato and green beans—the true, classic version of Genoese pesto known as "avvantaggiato".

FOR 1 FOCACCIA

100 g (3.5 oz) of fed starter
300 g (2 & ⅓ cups) all-purpose or Italian type '0' flour
180 ml (just over ¾ cup) water
50 ml (¼ cup) extra virgin olive oil
150 g (5.3 oz) green beans
50 g (1.75 oz) potatoes
around 20 basil leaves
1 tsp salt

FOR THE TOPPING
50 g (1.75 oz) parmesan cheese, cubed

Peel and boil the potatoes. Mash until smooth and let cool. Wash and steam the green beans. Let cool and cut into small pieces.
In the meantime, make the dough. Dissolve the starter in the water, then add the flour and begin to knead.
Once the dough has formed, add all the other ingredients, including the cooled vegetables and the salt.
Keep working the dough until it is smooth and elastic. Let rise in a covered bowl for around 4-5 hours, until doubled in volume.
Do a series of clock folds. Press the dough out with your hands onto a baking sheet lined with baking paper, using a bit of oil if needed to assist, to a thickness of about 1-1.5 cm (.5 in). Let rest for about another 2 hours.
Top the focaccia with the cubed parmesan and bake in an oven preheated to 250°C/480°F for around 20 minutes.

SPELT FLOUR *PANZEROTTI* WITH STEWED PEPPERS AND OREGANO

In summertime, bell peppers reach their peak flavor and oregano is in full season.
Born from this very summery idea, these panzerotti are meant to be eaten
slightly warm, with your hands, accompanied by a chilled beer.

FOR **6** PIECES

100 g (3.5 oz) of fed starter
300 g (3 cups) white spelt flour
150 ml (⅔ cup) water
30 ml (2 & ¼ tbsp) extra virgin olive oil
1 tsp salt

FOR THE FILLING

1 yellow bell pepper
1 red bell pepper
1 tbsp dried oregano
Extra virgin olive oil

Dissolve the starter in a bowl with the water and begin to add the spelt flour, kneading carefully. About halfway through the kneading, add the remaining ingredients. Continue to work the dough until smooth and homogeneous.
Let rise in a covered bowl for around 4-5 hours.
In the meantime, wash and deseed the peppers and cut into cubes. Cook in a covered pan with a bit of extra virgin olive oil and the oregano until soft. Let cool.
Once leavened, divide the dough into 6 ball shapes each weighing approximately 100 g (3.5 oz). On a floured work surface, roll each piece out with a rolling pin to a round sheet about 15 cm (6 in) in diameter.
Place a generous spoonful of the cooked peppers on one side of each sheet of dough. Fold over the dough to close the *panzerotto* and seal the edges well by pressing down with moistened fingers, then again with the tines of a fork.
Arrange the *panzerotti* on a baking sheet lined with baking paper. Let rest about an hour.
Heat the oven to 200°C/390°F. Brush the surfaces of each *panzerotto* with a small amount of extra virgin olive oil and bake for 20 minutes. Enjoy while still warm.

PANZEROTTI WITH BUTTERNUT SQUASH AND CARAMELIZED ONION

In Autumn, our house is never without butternut squash and onions on hand. This filling here combines the two, resulting in sweet and sour notes that are absolutely delicious inside these panzerotti.

FOR **5** PIECES

80 g (2.8 oz) of fed starter
260 g (2 cups) all-purpose or Italian
   type '0' flour
140 ml (just under ⅔ cup) water
30 ml (2 & ¼ tbsp) extra virgin olive oil
1 tsp salt

FOR THE FILLING

1 red onion
100 g (3.5 oz) butternut squash
1 tsp balsamic vinegar
Extra virgin olive oil

Prepare the filling: Peel the squash. Open and remove the seeds. Cut into small cubes. Peel and finely slice the onion. Add some olive oil to a pan and cook the vegetables. When just cooked, add the vinegar and reduce and continue cooking until caramelized. Let cool.

In the meantime, dissolve the starter in the water. Add the flour and begin to knead. Halfway through kneading, add the salt and the oil, and continue working the dough until homogeneous and elastic.

Let rise in a covered bowl for about 4-5 hours, until doubled in volume.

Divide the dough into 5 equal parts weighing about 100 g (3.5 oz) each.

Press each dough ball with your hands to form a thin disc about 10 cm (4 in) in diameter. Brush the edges with water and place a spoonful of the caramelized squash and onion filling in the middle of each disc. Fold the disk and close to form a half moon shape.

Brush the surfaces with a bit of oil and place the *panzerotti* on a baking sheet lined with baking paper.

Let rest for another two hours. Bake in an oven preheated to 200°C/390°F for around 20 minutes.

SEMI-WHOLE WHEAT NEAPOLITAN PIZZA

I have always loved pizza, ever since as a boy I'd go with my great-grandfather in the late afternoon to the neighborhood pizzeria for a slice of delicious sausage and four cheese pizza. The sun would still be out as we left the pizzeria, so there was time for a trip to the park just by our house. That was a long time ago, and many things have transpired in the meantime: recipes, experiences, desires and knowledge. Things may change, but pizza is always pizza.

FOR **3** PIECES

25 g (.9 oz) of fed starter
430 g (3 & ½ cups) all-purpose or
    Italian type '1' flour
280 ml (just over 1 cup) water
2 tsp salt

FOR DUSTING
Semolina flour

FOR THE TOPPING
1 can of peeled tomatoes
1 cow's milk mozzarella
Extra virgin olive oil
Salt

Dissolve the starter in the water and add the flour a little at a time. Begin to work the dough with your hands. Towards the end of kneading, add the salt and continue working until a well-combined, elastic dough forms.

Let rest about 30 minutes. Divide the dough into three parts weighing approximately 270 g (10 oz) each.

Work each piece with a series of clock folds to form a ball shape. Place in a plastic container with a lid and let rise at room temperature for 24 hours (ideally at a room temp of around 24-26 C°/75-79°F).

After rising, the pizza dough is now ready to be rolled out and topped.

In the meantime, make the sauce. Process the peeled tomatoes through a food mill and season with a bit of extra virgin olive oil and a pinch of salt. Slice the mozzarella and place in a colander to drain off the liquid.

Set the oven temperature to its highest, usually 250-270°C (480-520°F). You could also use a pizza stone if you have one.

Turn out the first dough ball onto a floured work surface (I recommend using semolina flour for this, which gives pizza an extra-nice crunch). Press the dough out with your hands with a circular movement, starting from the center and moving outwards towards the edges, until about 25 cm in diameter (10 in).

Be careful not to smash the air bubbles that will have formed in the dough.

Transfer the pizza to a baking sheet (or pizza peel if you are baking on a stone) and top with the tomato sauce.

Bake on the middle rack for about 5-10 minutes, until the edges are nicely puffed up. Remove from the oven and add the mozzarella. Return to the oven and bake for another few minutes. Add other toppings like olives, capers, and anchovy, according to taste.

A professional wood-fired oven usually can reach temperatures above 300°C/570°F (some even reach 350°C/660°F). And it is thanks to these extremely high temps that pizza cooks quickly and produces such great results. Recreating such conditions in home cooking is not easy, given that your average home oven cannot reach temperatures above 250°C/480°F.

Ovens made especially for pizza cooking do exist (electric or gas). Given their compact shape and the materials used, these ovens are able to reach higher temperatures.

Alternatively, use a baking stone in a regular home oven. Heat the stone in the oven as long as needed. Use a pizza peel to transfer the pizza (already topped) to the stone. With the heat being more evenly distributed and the temperature of the stone much higher than a still-cool baking sheet, the pizza will cook better and produce a nicer texture.

NO-KNEAD PIZZA WITH CHICORY GREENS AND *CACIOCAVALLO*

It takes about 15 minutes to make this dough, which is then let to rest in the refrigerator for an entire day. That's where the magic happens: the dough will rise very slowly, becoming soft and elastic. The next day, the well-leavened dough only needs to be pressed out onto a baking sheet and topped with your favorite ingredients (try the chicory greens and caciocavallo cheese here). Enjoy while still warm.

FOR A ROUND BAKING SHEET
30 CM (**12** IN) IN DIAMETER

60 g (2 oz) of fed starter
200 g (1 & ⅔ cups) semi-whole wheat
    flour
140 ml (just under ⅔ cup) water
1 tsp salt

FOR THE TOPPING
50 g (1.75 oz) chicory greens, sauteed
    with red chili pepper
50 g (1.75 oz) aged *caciocavallo* cheese,
    sliced into shavings
Extra virgin olive oil

In a large enough bowl, dissolve the starter in the water. Let rest about ten minutes and then add the flour and the salt, stirring briskly with your hands or a wooden spoon for a few minutes until well combined.

Cover the bowl with plastic wrap and poke holes in the wrap with a toothpick. Place in the refrigerator for an entire day.

The next day, grease the surface of a baking sheet with your hands. With your hands still greased, turn the dough out onto the sheet.

Let the dough rest another couple of hours. Delicately press the dough out to cover the entire surface of the sheet.

Then let rest another hour circa. Bake at 250°C/480°F for about 20 minutes.

Remove from the oven and top with the cooked chicory greens and return to the oven to bake for another 5 minutes. Finish with the *caciocavallo* cheese shavings when the pizza is just out of the oven.

WHOLE GRAIN SPELT FLOUR
AND TALEGGIO CHEESE *SCHIACCIATA*

The warm, melting taleggio atop this schiacciata flatbread releases wonderful fragrance, becoming very creamy, while the crust remains crunchy and flaky and the insides full of the aroma of whole wheat spelt. The effect is like being in the mountains come Sunday afternoon, with a slice of this delicious schiacciata, fresh from the oven.

FOR 1 SCHIACCIATA

200 g (7 oz) of fed starter
500 g (5 cups) whole grain spelt flour
280 ml (just over 1 cup) water
150 g (5 oz) taleggio cheese
1 tsp salt

Dissolve the starter in the water in a bowl. Pour in the spelt flour and begin to knead. About halfway through kneading, add the salt and knead well until a homogeneous dough forms.

Cover with a tea towel and let rise at room temperature for about 5 hours. Meanwhile cut the taleggio into thin slices and remove the rind.

Once the dough is leavened, divide it into two equal parts and press out one half onto a greased baking sheet. Evenly arrange the cheese slices on top, leaving a 1-cm (.4 in) border. Next roll out the second half of the dough and carefully place on top of the first half to cover it completely. Seal the edges with a bit of water.

Let rest for about another two hours. Bake in an oven preheated to 200°C/390°F for around 30 minutes.

HOLIDAYS AND SPECIAL OCCASIONS

Sometimes bread can tell more stories than words. The softness of a dough, the unique ingredients and special touches, the methods and attention given to creating a loaf of homemade bread to set on the table—at these times, bread can express more affection than one can convey with pen and paper...

CHESTNUT AND THYME MORSELS

Bringing together the sweetness of chestnuts, the pungency of thyme and the colors of fall foliage, these little bites of autumn flavors are a great snack to take along your country walks, or while wandering the streets of downtown. With a bit of drizzle outside, I'd add a nice glass of warm wine.

FOR **25** PIECES

100 g (3.5 oz) of fed starter
350 g (2 & ¾ cups) all-purpose or
    Italian type '0' flour
150 ml (⅔ cup) water
100 g (3.5 oz) boiled chestnuts
50 ml (¼ cup) extra virgin olive oil
1 tsp salt
1 tsp dried thyme

Process the boiled chestnuts with a food mill until smooth. Let cool.

Dissolve the starter in a bowl with the water. Add the flour and chestnut puree and being to work the dough with your hands.

Next add the thyme, salt, and oil and continue kneading well until a homogeneous and elastic dough forms.

Let rise at room temperature in a covered bowl for about 5-6 hours, until doubled in volume.

Transfer to a floured work surface and do a series of folds. Shape into balls weighing approximately 30 g (1 oz) each. Arrange on a baking sheet lined with baking paper. Let rest for another couple of hours. Bake in an oven preheated to 180°C/355°F for about 20 minutes.

CROWN LOAF WITH SAGE

This round loaf is simple yet fragrant, perfect for a family lunch. It makes for a lovely table centerpiece, too, where guests can break off chunks of bread while waiting for the roast and potatoes to arrive—in Italy, classic Sunday dishes are also typically seasoned with sage.

FOR 1 CROWN LOAF

140 g (5 oz) of fed starter

450 g (3 & ⅔ cups) all-purpose or
    Italian type '0' flour

230 ml (just under 1 cup) water

30 g (2 & ¼ tbsp) extra virgin olive oil

2 tsp salt

FOR THE FILLING

Extra virgin olive oil

About 30 leaves of fresh sage

Mix the starter in the water until dissolved almost completely. Add the flour and begin to combine with your hands.

Next add the oil and the salt, continuing to work thoroughly until a very elastic and smooth dough forms.

Let rise at room temperature in a covered bowl for 5-6 hours.

Turn the dough out onto a floured work surface. Do a series of book folds and press out the dough with your hands to a rectangle sheet 1 cm (.4 in) thick.

Brush the dough with a bit of oil and spread the sage leaves on top, trying to cover the entire surface.

Roll the square up from its long side to form a rolled loaf. Then close the ends to form a crown shape.

Carefully transfer to a baking sheet lined with baking paper. Cover with a humid tea towel and let rest for another 2-3 hours.

Score the entire surface with small cross cuts and bake at 200°C/390°F for 40-50 minutes.

DANUBIO ROLLS WITH ARTICHOKES AND *FOSSA* CHEESE

Danubio is one of those breads suited to Sunday lunches, special occasions, or jaunts into the countryside. It's a bread meant for sharing, for nibbling on with friends and family, enjoying each bite's small, tasty surprise inside. Children will fight over it, down to the last piece.

FOR ABOUT **20** BALL SHAPES

150 g (5.3 oz) of fed starter
450 g (3 & ⅔ cups) all-purpose or
    Italian type '0' flour
100 ml (⅓ cup) water
100 ml (⅓ cup) milk
70 g (⅓ cup) butter, softened
50 g (6 tbsp) unrefined cane sugar
1 egg
2 tsp salt

FOR THE FILLING
1 large artichoke
50 g (1.75 oz) *fossa*-aged cheese,
    thinly sliced
Extra virgin olive oil
1 small garlic clove
Fresh mint leaves
Salt and pepper

TO DECORATE
1 egg yolk
2 tbsp milk

Dissolve the starter in the water. Add the flour and begin to knead.

Add the remaining ingredients and lastly the salt. Knead rigorously until a soft and homogeneous dough forms.

Let rise at room temperature in a covered bowl for about 4-5 hours.

In the meantime, make the filling.

Clean and thinly slice the artichoke. Saute in a pan with a drizzle of olive oil, the garlic (peeled and smashed) and the mint until the veg is soft and the liquid has cooked off. Adjust for salt and pepper and let cool. Next add the cheese and combine.

Turn the dough out onto a floured work surface. Form ball shapes weighing approximately 40 g each (1.5 oz) and fill each ball with a bit of the artichoke mixture.

Line a round baking sheet 30 cm in diameter (12 in) with baking paper and arrange the balls inside, leaving space between them.

Beat the egg with the milk and brush onto the surfaces. Let rise for another two hours, until nearly doubled in volume.

Heat the oven to 200°C/390°F and bake for around 30 minutes.

RUSTIC WALNUT LOAVES

There's an old saying from the countryside around Bologna that speaks to the at once "rich" and "poor" associations walnut bread evokes—rich for peasants who live off the land, yet poor for those with the means to eat a more plentiful or sophisticated diet. In any case, this bread is certainly rich in flavor, and is meant for festivities or to perk you up on a rainy day. It's even better served with a nice goat's milk robiola cheese.

FOR **3** PIECES

150 g (5.3 oz) of fed starter
500 g (5 cups) white spelt flour
250 ml (1 cup) water
100 g (3.5 oz) shelled walnuts
2 tsp salt

Coarsely chop the walnuts.

Dissolve the starter in the water. Add the spelt flour and begin to knead.

Shortly after, add the walnuts and the salt, continuing to work the dough until the consistency is very elastic and not sticky.

Let rise in a covered bowl for 4-5 hours, until doubled in size.

Re-work the dough by doing a series of clock folds. Shape into three loaves weighing about 300-350 g (10.5-12.5 oz) each.

Arrange the rounds on a baking sheet lined with baking paper and let rest for another couple hours.

Heat the oven to 250°C/480°F. Dust the loaves with a bit of flour and score with a triangle cut. Bake for 25-30 minutes, the first 10 at 250°C/480°F and the remaining at 200°C/390°F.

SOFT BUTTERNUT SQUASH BREAD

In the Padana plains of Italy, locals eagerly anticipate the arrival of autumn, as this is squash season, when the fields come alive with the orange colors of this most versatile product (even in a foggy area like this one). The cooked butternut squash used in this dough gives the bread a lovely fall color and rustic fragrance, and a flavor that is sweet but not overly so.

FOR 1 LOAF

150 g (5.3 oz) of fed starter
500 g (4 cups) all-purpose or Italian
    type '0' flour
200 ml (⅓ pt) water
100 g (3.5 oz) cleaned butternut squash
50 ml (¼ cup) extra virgin olive oil
2 tsp salt

Cut the squash into small pieces and roast at 180°C/355°F. Mash with a fork or process through a food mill and let cool.

In the meantime, mix the starter in a bowl with the water. Add the flour and begin to knead using your hands.

Halfway through kneading, add the mashed squash, oil, and salt and continue working the dough until it is homogeneous. (The dough will be soft and could be a little sticky.)

Let rise in a covered bowl for 5-6 hours, until doubled in volume.

Turn the dough out onto a floured work surface. Do a series of book folds and shape into a loaf. Carefully transfer to a plum cake loaf tin lined with baking paper. Let rise for another couple of hours. Bake for around an hour in an oven preheated to 180°C/355°F.

CACIO & PEPE PANBRIOCHE

I waited nearly 30 years of my life to taste a cacio e pepe worthy of its name. Here, the flavor pairing of cheese and black pepper which made the dish famous takes a lead role in panbrioche (and in my memories): spiced, aromatic, salty, semi-sweet. Delicious.

FOR 1 PANBRIOCHE LOAF

100 g (3.5oz) of fed starter

350 g (2 & ¾ cups) all-purpose or
   Italian type '0' flour

85 ml (just under ⅓ pt) water

100 ml (⅓ cup) milk

50 ml (¼ cup) extra virgin olive oil

50 g (½ cup) grated pecorino romano
   cheese

1 egg

1 tsp salt

1 tsp coarsely ground black pepper

TO DECORATE

1 egg

1 tsp coarsely ground black pepper

Dissolve the starter in a bowl with the water and the milk. Add the flour and begin to knead. Once the consistency is smooth, add the remaining ingredients and continue working the dough until well-combined. This could be challenging, but it's important to persevere with the kneading to create a panbrioche as soft and fluffy as possible.

Let rise in a bowl covered with a tea towel for about 4-5 hours.

Transfer the dough to a floured work surface. Do a series of folds and shape into a loaf. Transfer to a plum cake loaf tin lined with baking paper and let rise again. Cover with cling wrap to prevent a crust from forming and leave to rest for at least two hours more.

In the meantime, heat the oven to 200°C/390°F. Beat the egg and carefully brush on the surface of the loaf, then sprinkle on plenty of ground black pepper.

Bake for around 30-35 minutes. Use a toothpick to check the readiness of the loaf.

SAVORY BRIOCHE LOAF WITH CARROT AND NUTMEG

Creating savory versions of the classic brioche loaf is easy, fun, and sure to bring great results. With the use of vegetables, juices, and spices, these soft, fragrant breads offer rich color and flavor. Serve them at an aperitif, or still warm for Sunday lunch.

FOR 1 BRIOCHE LOAF

75 g (2.65 oz) of fed starter
250 g (2 & ½ cups) white spelt flour
150 ml (⅔ cup) carrot juice
75 g (⅓ cup) soy yogurt
25 ml (2 tbsp) extra virgin olive oil
2 tsp ground nutmeg
1 tsp salt

TO DECORATE
2 tsp ground nutmeg

Dissolve the starter in the carrot juice at room temperature. Add the spelt flour and begin to knead. Next add the soy yogurt, oil, nutmeg, and salt.
Work thoroughly to obtain a dough as homogeneous and elastic as possible.
Let rise in a covered bowl for about 5-6 hours, until doubled in volume.
Work the dough again with a series of folds on a floured work surface. Divide the dough into two equal parts and shape into loaves slightly longer than your plum cake loaf tin. Braid the two loaves together and place inside the tin lined with baking paper.
Let rise another two or three hours. Dust the surface with the nutmeg and bake in an oven heated to 200°C/390°F for 30-40 minutes circa.

TEA BREAD

Years ago when I was younger, I was really crazy about tea. I loved the ritual of it, the objects involved, and the minimalism. This bread is now a tribute to the world of tea, just as warm, simple, and essential.

FOR 1 LOAF

200 g (7 oz) of fed starter
700 g (5 & ¾ cups) whole grain,
    stone-ground flour
500 ml (2 cups) black tea
1 tbsp unrefined cane sugar
2 tsp salt

Brew the tea. Sweeten with sugar and let cool to room temperature.
Dissolve the starter in the tea. Slowly add the flour as you start to knead. When the dough is well hydrated and homogeneous, cover and let rest for 5-6 hours, until doubled in volume.
Turn the dough out onto a floured work surface and do a series of clock folds to form a round loaf.
Cover with a tea towel and let rise again for a couple hours more.
Score the surface of the loaf with a very sharp knife. Lightly flour the loaf and bake in an oven heated to 250°C/480°F for the first 10 minutes, then lower the heat to 180°C/355°F and bake for another 40-50 minutes.

PILSNER AND MUSTARD LOAF

Aside from bread, I enjoy making other products at home, like beer, for instance. My efforts have brought me great satisfaction, which might be due to the craft of fermentation and its role in both bread and beer—from the maniacal attention to detail required to the unconditional love that comes with making things all on your own. For these reasons, using beer as an ingredient in bread makes perfect sense. And why not a touch of mustard powder as well?

FOR 1 LOAF

150 g (5.3 oz) of fed starter
400 g (3 & ⅓ cups) whole wheat flour
200 ml (⅓ pt) Pilsner or similar beer
1 tsp salt
2 tsp mustard powder

TO DECORATE
1 tsp mustard powder

Dissolve the starter in the (room temperature) beer and add the flour. Knead with your hands. Halfway through kneading add the salt and the mustard powder.
When the dough is elastic and very homogeneous, let rise in a covered bowl for 5-6 hours.
Do a series of folds on a floured work surface and shape into a loaf. Cover and let rise again for two hours on a baking sheet lined with baking paper.
Just before baking, lightly moisten the surface of the loaf and dust with the mustard powder.
Bake at 250°C/480°F for the first 10 minutes, then lower the heat to 200°C/390°F and bake for another 30 minutes circa.

POLENTA AND CHEESE LOAF

Corn and cheese pair very well, as polenta concia—polenta blended with cheese and other dairy products, possibly butter—demonstrates. From this came the brilliant idea of creating a bread from the same ingredients. The result went beyond all expectation: a crunchy crust, with melting cheese inside. A match made in heaven!

FOR 1 LOAF

100 g (3.5 oz) of fed starter

200 g (1 & ⅔ cups) coarse cornmeal flour

200 g (1 & ⅔ cups) all-purpose or Italian type '0' flour

200 ml (⅓ pt) water

100 g (3.5 oz) alpeggio (or similar) cheese, cubed

2 tsp salt

Dissolve the starter in the water and slowly add the flours. Knead thoroughly for about ten minutes. Next add the salt and the cubed cheese and continue working until a smooth, homogeneous dough forms.

Let rise in a covered bowl for 4-5 hours, until doubled in size.

Work the dough on a floured work surface with a series of book folds and shape into a loaf. Let rise another two hours.

Score and bake in an oven heated to 250°C/480°F for 15 minutes, then bake for another 30 minutes at 200°C/390°F.

SOFT SESAME SEED HAMBURGER BUNS

Once you have tried these buns, they will never be missing from your freezer. Make about a dozen of them, to have ready on hand when you feel like relaxing on the couch with a beer, in the company of friends. Soft, tasty, sure to satisfy and above all healthy, they also go well with veggie or bean burgers.

FOR **6** PIECES

FOR THE MILK ROUX
15 g (2 tbsp) all-purpose or Italian type '0' flour
75 ml (between ¼ and ⅓ cup) milk

FOR THE DOUGH
The prepared milk roux
80 g (2.7 oz) of fed starter
220 g (1 & ⅓ cups) all-purpose or Italian type '0' flour
50 g (1/3 cup) rice flour
140 ml (just under ⅔ cup) water
15 g (1 tbsp) agave syrup
15 ml (1 tbsp) extra virgin olive oil
3 tsp sesame seeds
1 tsp salt

TO DECORATE
2 tbsp milk
2 tsp sesame seeds

Combine the milk and flour in a small pot until a homogeneous batter forms.
Transfer to the stove top and continue stirring while heating until the batter reaches a temperature of around 65°C/150°F (use a small food thermometer; lacking this, remove the roux from the heat as soon as it begins to thicken and take on a translucent color).
Cover the pot with cling wrap to prevent the surface from drying out. Let cool.
Dissolve the starter in the water in a bowl. Add the cooled milk roux, the flours, and the agave syrup. Begin to knead.
Halfway through kneading add the salt, the sesame seeds, and the extra virgin olive oil. Combine thoroughly.
Cover and let rise at room temperature for about 5 hours.
Transfer the dough to a floured work surface and do a series of folds. Let rest again for 30 minutes. Shape into six loaves weighing approximately 100 g (3.5 oz) each.
Let rise for a couple of hours. While the oven is preheating to 180°C/355°F, carefully brush the surfaces of the buns with the milk and generously sprinkle with the sesame seeds.
Bake for about 20-25 minutes. Use a toothpick to check the readiness.

RYE AND FONTINA CHEESE ROLL

Rye breads and mountain cheeses are made for each other, and here they are together again in this rolled loaf. I suggest cutting the roll into slices while still warm, perhaps accompanied by some rustic salami from the mountains.

FOR 1 ROLL

200 g (7 oz) of fed starter
400 g (3 & ¼ cups) all-purpose or
    Italian type '0' flour
400 g (3 & ⅛ cups) rye flour
400 ml (1 & ⅓ cups) water
100 g (3.5 oz) valdostana fontina cheese
    or similar
1 tbsp extra virgin olive oil
2 tsp salt

Dissolve the starter in the water. Add the flours, kneading well with your hands. Halfway through kneading, add the salt and the oil, and continue working the dough into a smooth, homogeneous ball shape.

Let rise in a covered bowl for 5-6 hours, until doubled in size.

Transfer the dough to a floured work surface. Do a cycle of folds. Use a rolling pin to roll the dough out to a rectangular sheet about 1 cm (.4 in) thick.

Cut the cheese into small cubes and cover the entire surface of the dough, leaving some space along the edges. Lightly moisten the edges with water. Roll the dough sheet up from its long side to form a rolled loaf.

Place the loaf on a baking sheet lined with baking paper and let rest another two hours circa. Bake in an oven preheated to 200°C/390°F for about 40 minutes.

SMOKED SPIRALS

I adore the flavors of Italy's Alto Adige region (if by chance that's not yet obvious!). With these spiral-shaped rolls, I have brought together some of my favorite ingredients and made sure every bite offers a delicious dose of them.

FOR **10** PIECES

75 g (2.65 oz) of fed starter
250 g (2 cups) all-purpose or Italian
  type '0' flour
125 ml (½ cup) water
50 g (¼ cup) butter, softened
1 tsp salt
1 tsp of chopped onion, garlic, chive
  and parsley

FOR THE FILLING
10 thin slices of smoked cheese
10 thin slices of speck

Dissolve the starter in the water. Add the flour and begin to knead.
When the dough is nearly formed, add the salt, butter, and the chopped herbs. At first, combining the butter with the dough will be a challenge, but keep working for about ten minutes and you will obtain a homogeneous dough.
Cover and let rise at room temperature for about 4 hours.
Turn the dough out onto a floured work surface. Do a series of folds. Use a rolling pin to roll out the dough to approximately 1 cm (.4 in) thickness. Cut out rectangular shapes about 3 cm wide by 15 cm (1.2 x 6 in) long.
Place a slice of speck and a slice of cheese lengthwise on the shape and roll up to form a small spiral. Place on a baking sheet lined with baking paper. Cover and let rise for another couple of hours. Bake in an oven preheated to 200°C/390°F for about 15 minutes.

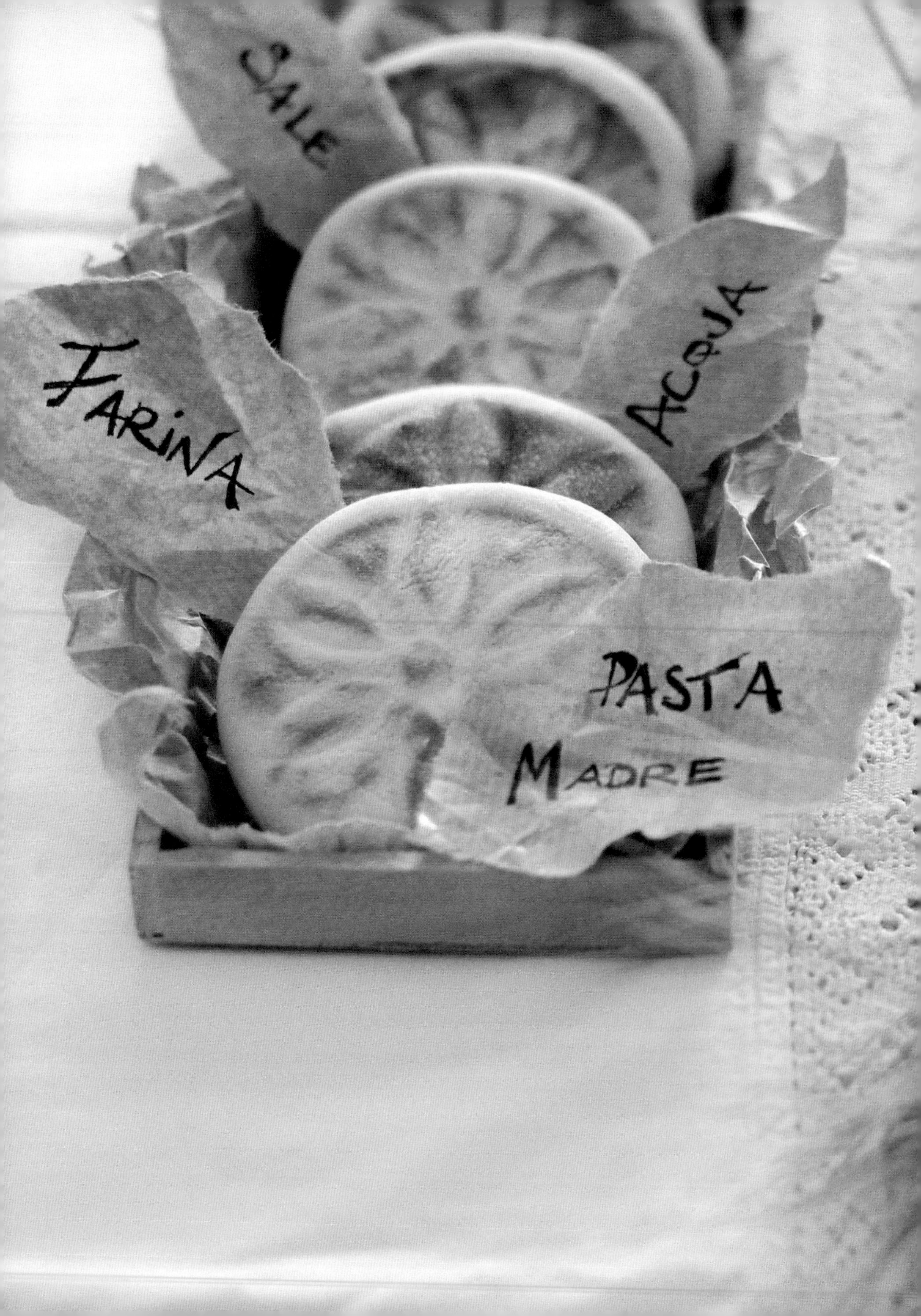
SALE
FARINA
ACQUA
PASTA MADRE

RUSTIC *TIGELLE* FLATBREADS

My friends from Modena will have something to say about these. "They're called crescentine, not tigelle!" they will say, referring to a longstanding battle over whether this peasant flatbread hails from the city or the mountains, from Bologna or Modena, and what it should rightly be called. Once seated around a table with tigelle, however, everyone agrees and gets along. Try them warm and topped with cured meats, cheeses or vegetables, together with a nice glass of Lambrusco wine. And maybe a game of cards.

FOR ABOUT **20** PIECES

150 g (5.3 oz) of fed starter
250 g (2 cups) all-purpose or Italian
    type '0' flour
250 ml (1 cup) milk
3 tbsp extra virgin olive oil
1 tsp malt
2 tsp salt

Dissolve the starter in the room temperature milk. Add the flour, malt, salt, and oil and continue working the dough until it is elastic and soft.

Cover with a tea towel and let rise for about 6 hours, until doubled in volume.

On a floured work surface, do a series of clock folks then roll the dough out with a rolling pin to a sheet about 1 cm (.4 in) thick.

Use a glass to form disc shapes in the dough the same size as the tins of the *tigelliera*. Cook over fire for three or four minutes on each side.

Enjoy them while still warm, topped with salamis, soft and aged cheeses, and vegetables.

SMOKED BLACK TEA CRUMPETS

When salted butter begins to melt on a still-warm crumpet, images of Victorian-era tea rooms come to mind, where the quiet is broken only by the sound of spoons against porcelain tea cups. This is one of the reasons I love London, without ever having been there.

FOR ABOUT 10 PIECES

100 g (3.5 oz) of fed starter
300 g (2 & ⅓ cups) all-purpose or
   Italian type '0' flour
350 ml (1 & ⅓ cups) smoked black tea
2 tsp baking soda
A pinch of salt

FOR COOKING

1 tbsp butter

Make the tea by steeping a spoonful of smoked black tea (like Lapsang Souchong) for four minutes in boiling water. Let cool.

Once the tea has reached room temp, add the starter to the tea and whisk or stir with a spoon. Add the flour and continue mixing until you have a semi-liquid batter.

Let rest in a covered bowl at room temperature for 4-5 hours.

Add the baking soda and the salt to the dough and combine thoroughly.

Heat a bit of butter in a pan on the stove. Using a ladle about 8 cm (3 in) in diameter, ladle a scoop of batter onto the center of the pan.

Cook for three minutes on each side, until the crumpet puffs up and takes on its characteristic bubbly surface.

Serve warm (or better still, lightly toasted) with salted butter and honey, or try the classic British way with scrambled eggs, soft cheese, and pickles.

CREAMY PEANUT BUTTER BREAD

Even I could not believe how delicious and fragrant this bread came out. Peanut butter is not exactly a common ingredient in breads, yet the result here is a surprisingly flavorful, semi-sweet, soft loaf to serve any time of day: for breakfast, afternoon snack, or even cocktail hour.

FOR 1 LOAF

100 g (3.5 oz) of fed starter
500 g (4 cups) all-purpose or Italian
    type '0' flour
300 ml (1 & ¼ cups) water
120 g (4 oz) peanut butter
25 g (1 tbsp) honey
2 tsp salt

Dissolve the starter in the water. Add the flour and the honey and begin to knead. Halfway through kneading add the salt and the peanut butter and work rigorously to completely combine the ingredients into the dough.

Let rise at room temperature in a covered bowl for about 5 hours.

When the dough has doubled, turn it out onto a floured work surface and do a series of clock folds. Shape the loaf as you prefer.

Transfer the loaf to a baking sheet lined with baking paper and let rise for another couple hours, covered. Bake in an oven preheated to 200°C/355°F for about 40 minutes.

MOCK *STOLLEN* CAKE

This interpretation of the classic German Christmas cake stollen brings with it all the lights, colors, biting cold and steaming, warm vin brulé of the season. Here the starter is combined with raisins, pine nuts, and marzipan, to get you in the holiday spirit.

FOR 1 *STOLLEN* CAKE

50 g (1.75 oz) of fed starter
200 g (1 & ⅓ cups) all-purpose or
   Italian type '0' flour
100 ml (⅓ cup) water
60 g (2 oz) marzipan (the chocolate-
   covered type also works)
1 tbsp pine nuts
1 tbsp raisins
1 tsp salt

FOR THE GLAZE
1 tsp water
1 tbsp powdered sugar

Dissolve the starter in the water. Add the flour, the raisins, the pine nuts, and the salt and begin to knead, working the dough until it is smooth and elastic. Cover in a bowl and let rise at room temperature for 5-6 hours.

Turn the dough out onto a floured work surface and do a series of book folds. Using a rolling pin, roll out the dough to a rectangular sheet measuring about 40 cm (16 in) on one side and the other the length of your marzipan piece.

Place the marzipan piece along the edge of the dough sheet and roll up the dough all the way to form a cylinder shape.

Close the ends by applying a bit of pressure. Place the stollen on a baking sheet lined with baking paper. Cover and let rise for another 2 hours circa.

Moisten the surface of the stollen with a small amount of water and dust with powdered sugar.

Bake in an oven preheated to 180°C/390°F for 25 minutes.

PINZA CHRISTMAS CAKE

Nearly forgotten today, the traditional Christmas dessert called pinza is still around thanks to classic Italian food texts like Ada Boni's The Talisman. *It belongs to a group of sweets classified as for "holidays only" given its laborious method and high calorie content.*

FOR 1 *PINZA*

150 g (5.3 oz) of fed starter
400 g (3 & ¼ cups) all-purpose or
   Italian type '0' flour
200 ml (⅓ pt) water
200 g (7 oz) apricot jam
75 g (⅓ cup) butter, softened
75 g (3.5 oz) dried figs
75 g blanched almonds, cut in half
40 g (1.4 oz) hazelnuts
35 g (1 oz) walnuts
25 g (¼ cup) cocoa powder
25 g (⅛ cup) raisins, soaked in rum

TO GLAZE
1 glass of rum
1 tbsp acacia flower honey

Knead the starter with the flour and water until a soft and homogeneous dough forms. Let rise in a large bowl for around 5 hours.

Add the other ingredients to the dough, one at a time, starting with the butter and the jam. Work the dough rigorously for a while, which might be difficult at first, until all the ingredients are completely combined.

Shape into a loaf and then close up to form a donut shape. Moisten the ends with water to help them stick together.

Place the ring on a baking sheet covered with baking paper and let rise for another 3 hours.

Bake in an oven preheated to 180°C/355°F for about 45-50 minutes.

In the meantime, heat the rum slightly, add the honey and dissolve. Remove the cake when done and brush the entire surface with the honeyed rum. Repeat the process several times (if possible, also on the days following) as to render the cake's surface glassy and soft.

TRADITIONAL *PANETTONE*

Italian panettone cake is the ultimate challenge for home bakers. Even more so than pizza or focaccia. Difficult to prepare at home, especially without a mixer, panettone remains nonetheless an essential recipe for home bakers or anyone who loves to bake. Yet when the dough begins to rise and expand during leavening, finally reaching the edge of the cake tin, the satisfaction is immeasurable. It's like waiting for Christmas to come, and finally experiencing the joy of gift-giving.

FOR ONE 1 KG (2.2 LBS) *PANETTONE*, OR TWO
WEIGHING 500 G (1.1 LBS) EACH

COMPLETE LIST OF INGREDIENTS
50 g (1.75 oz) of fed starter
350 g (2 & ¾ cups) all-purpose or
   Italian type '0' flour (if possible,
   "strong")
160 ml (just over ⅔ cup) water
120 g (1/2 cup) butter
140 g (5 oz) raisins
120 g (½ cup) unrefined cane sugar
100 g (3.5 oz) candied orange peel,
   cubed
4 egg yolks
Seeds of 1 vanilla pod
1 tsp salt

FOR THE FIRST DOUGH
50 g (1.75 oz) of fed starter
150 g (1 & ¼ cup) all-purpose or Italian
   type '0' flour (if possible, "strong")
65 ml (just over ¼ cup) water
40 g (5 tbsp) unrefined cane sugar
20 g (1 & ⅓ tbsp) butter, softened

FOR THE SECOND DOUGH
Dough made previously
150 g (1 & ¼ cup) all-purpose or Italian
   type '0' flour (if possible, "strong")
65 ml (just over ¼ cup) water
60 g (5 tbsp) unrefined cane sugar
40 g (2 & ¾ tbsp) butter, softened
A pinch of salt

THE FIRST DOUGH

Dissolve the starter in the water. Add the flour and the sugar, mixing with your hands or a spoon. Add the softened butter and continue working the dough until smooth and homogeneous. Let rise in a covered bowl at a temperature of around 20°C/68°F for about 12 hours.

THE SECOND DOUGH

Add the following ingredients to the first dough, in this order: half of the water (30 ml or ⅛ cup), the flour, the sugar, and the butter. Knead vigorously for a few minutes, until all the ingredients are well absorbed into the dough.
Dissolve the salt in the remaining water (30 ml or ⅛ cup) and add to the dough. Knead again and let rise in a bowl at 25°C/77°F for another 12 hours circa.

THIRD AND FINAL DOUGH

Add only the flour and the vanilla to the dough made previously. Knead until the dough is elastic and stretches well.
Now add the egg yolks, kneading and stretching the dough.
Add the water, continuing to knead until the dough stretches well.
Cream the softened butter and add to the dough. Knead again until the dough is smooth, elastic and homogeneous.
Lastly, add the raisins and the candied orange zest, kneading and stretching to combine all the ingredients.
Let rest for about 30 minutes at room temperature.
At this point, if you want to make two smaller panettone, divide the dough into two equal parts.
Turn the dough out onto a work surface. Using both hands, shape two perfectly round ball loaves (the technique is called pirlare in Italian).
Transfer the loaves to a tin made for panettone cakes and let rise directly on the baking sheet for 18 hours at 25°C/77°F, until the dough reaches the top edge of the tin.

FOR THE THIRD AND FINAL DOUGH

The dough made previously

50 g (⅓ cup) all-purpose or Italian type '0' flour (if possible, "strong")

30 ml (⅛ cup) water

60 g (4 tbsp) butter, softened

140 g (5 oz) raisins

100 g (3.5 oz) candied orange peel, cubed

4 egg yolks

20 g (3 tbsp) unrefined cane sugar

Seeds of 1 vanilla pod

A pinch of salt

During this phase, try not to move the loaves to avoid disturbing the leavening process and causing the dough to collapse.

Bake in an oven preheated to 180°C/355°F for 50 minutes (35 minutes if you have made two smaller cakes), without opening the oven door during the first phase of cooking.

Remove from the oven and let cool upside down, suspended from a hanging apparatus (using dowels or similar). Leave for 12 hours. If you are not going to eat the panettone right away, store it in a plastic food bag, well sealed.

SUMMARY OF LEAVENING TIMES AND TEMPERATURES

	Kneading time	Leavening times	Ideal leavening temperature
First dough	30 minutes	12 hours	20°C/68°F
Second dough	30 minutes	12 hours	25°C/77°F
Third and final dough	2 hours	18 hours	25°C/77°F

"STRONG" FLOUR

Long rising times, a dough's richness, and the amount of ingredients are all factors that put flours to a test (not to mention home bakers). At times, using weaker flours with lower gluten content results in a dough that cannot hold up to stress factors and thus doesn't leaven well. This leads to a flat panettone, with poor elasticity and a consistency that crumbles as soon as it's sliced.

So-called "strong" flours are recommended for just this reason in recipes like panettone and most other leavened holiday or special occasion cakes, flours such as Manitoba (which was once even labeled "for panettone"). You can find strong flours that are also organic and stone-ground, always preferable to industrial, refined, nutrient-poor flours.

DOUGH STRETCH

The term stretch perfectly describes how a dough, one worked vigorously, consistently, with attention and dedication, is able to absorb all the ingredients, water and fats included, to become strong and elastic.

At first, especially for those not yet accustomed to it, adding semi-liquid ingredients (egg yolks, softened butter, etc.) to an already formed dough can seem very difficult, if not impossible. The trick is to not lose hope, not to panic, but rather to persist in working the dough consistently for several minutes until all the ingredients start to come together and combine. Naturally, a bread mixer can be a very useful tool in this process.

TABLE OF CONTENTS

RECIPES

INDEX

ACKNOWLEDGMENTS

Writing a cookbook is a truly collective experience. Collective because the book will eventually end up in the homes, hearts, and stomachs of all those who wish to experience this flour- and bread-scented dream of mine, sourdough. So it is those people I must thank first.

It's a collective experience also thanks to the people who contributed to this book's creation, who kneaded along with me, who took photographs, who tried recipes using their critical (and some less critical) sense of taste, who played with flour and ran about the kitchen while I worked meticulously on breadmaking and studied photographic exposure and light.

Thank you to my entire family. Without each and every one of them, this book would not even have gotten started. It is with them I would like to share, in equal parts, every complement (and every criticism, naturally).

A special thank you goes to Benedetta and the precious help she gave me in sorting out difficult moments during the crafting of this book, in particular towards the end when it was ready to go to press.

And endless thanks to those who gave me the opportunity to work on this project. Alessandra, Giusy, Guido and Tommaso and the entire editorial staff, all truly lovely, passionate, strong people, full of stories and the desire to do good. You have guided me along this new path, and I hope we will follow many more together in the future.

© Guido Tommasi Editore – Datanova S.r.l., 2018

Text: Riccardo Astolfi
Photographs: © Chiara Frascari and © Benedetta Marchi, pages 46, 49, 55, 76, 84-85, 96, 100, 103, 111, 116-117, 120, 125, 131, 148, 152, 178-179, 185, 189, 198, 201, 205, 209, 222, 225, 226
Graphics: Tommaso Bacciocchi
Translation: Amy Gulick
Editorial: Anita Ravasio

ISBN: 978 88 6753 246 9

Printed in Italy